Famous Biographies for Young People

FAMOUS AMERICAN
WOMEN ATHLETES

BOOKS BY HELEN HULL JACOBS

Adventure in Bluejeans
Modern Tennis
Improve Your Tennis
"By Your Leave, Sir"
Beyond the Game
Barry Cort
Laurel for Judy
Tennis
Storm against the Wind
Judy, Tennis Ace
Center Court
Golf, Swimming and Tennis
Proudly She Serves!
The Young Sportsman's Guide to Tennis
Famous American Women Athletes

FAMOUS AMERICAN
WOMEN ATHLETES

by Helen Hull Jacobs

ILLUSTRATED WITH PHOTOGRAPHS

Dodd, Mead & Company · New York

TO VIRGINIA GURNEE

ACKNOWLEDGMENTS

In the preparation of this book, a great deal of personal information about the famous athletes of whom I was writing was needed. To the athletes themselves, or in some cases, to their families or friends, I am indebted for the fullest cooperation.

In the case of every sport represented, the United States Olympic Association, the Amateur Athletic Union and the other amateur, as well as professional, associations and congresses that govern them, have provided me with the necessary information that is not in the record books.

To all of them I give my thanks. I hope that the result of my work and their assistance will add something to the story of great women in sport.

Helen Hull Jacobs

New York City

FOREWORD

Helen Jacobs was my first tennis heroine. She probably didn't have the finest strokes in the game, but she had much more: the ability to work and fight and to come from behind with a hidden strength to win.

In the four major matches I played against Helen, I felt I had to always play at my very best to win. In our semifinal at Wimbledon in 1938—incidentally the last amateur match I lost—Helen was unbeatable. I felt I played extremely well, yet she won handily, 6-4, 6-4. For the first time in my tennis career in championship play, I could not feel badly about losing, for I lost to a superior player on that day.

On my first trip to Europe as a member of the Wightman Cup team, of which Helen was captain, I collapsed on the center court of the Roland Garros stadium. Though concerned with her own matches and the welfare of the team, Helen made daily trips to see me in the hospital, bringing thoughtful gifts and worlds of encouragement to a nineteen-year-old who had been given word that she would never play tennis again. I shall never forget what a warm, kind human being Helen Jacobs was when I needed help so desperately.

It is always difficult to analyze an opponent's game, or to tell how great she was. Helen's first service was aggressive; she had a safe, accurate second service with enough spin to be troublesome, especially on grass. Her backhand was hit flat and she could pass her opponent on both sides with equal ease. One heard rumors of her weaker forehand because she reverted to a slice in tight matches. It was, however, extremely well hit; low and deep and a very difficult shot to handle on the soft grass courts. She was not a net rusher but could handle herself very well at the net, as is obvious by the number of doubles titles she held.

To me, her greatness lies in her fine tactical mind, her never-say-die attitude and her ability to scramble. In my estimation, she must be ranked in the first five of the greatest women players I have witnessed in my long tennis career.

Helen was plagued with injuries during much of her career, though she managed, with the same determination that she showed on the courts, to overcome them and be the fine champion that she was: to win the national championships four years running, which record has not been duplicated by any other American woman player.

Helen Jacobs has had a varied career. She holds the distinction of having been presented at the Court of St. James; she is the author of sixteen fine books—fiction and nonfiction; she has designed sports clothes here and in England; and served as a Wave in World War II and the Korean War. At present, she is a Commander in the Naval Reserve and is a senior editor on the BOOK OF KNOWLEDGE staff at Grolier Incorporated, in New York. As recently as 1962, I met a woman who served under her during the war and she had only the finest praise for Helen Jacobs.

Helen Hull Jacobs was my most difficult opponent on the tennis court and as fine a friend as I have ever had. I know you will enjoy this, her latest book, and I look forward to adding it to all the others that she has written.

Alice Marble

CONTENTS

PHOTOGRAPHIC SUPPLEMENT

Alice Marble was one of the greatest volleyers of all the women champions. Here she goes for a low one on the backhand.

The incomparable "Babe" Didrikson drives to the green.

United Press International, Inc.

Aileen Riggin shows perfect style in this swan dive.

Style, timing and power were Ann Curtis Cuneo's greatest assets.

United Press International, Inc.

Carol Heiss does compulsory figures at Squaw Valley. No skater had finer grace or balance than this world champion.

Wide World Photos

Gretchen Fraser skis in the grand style to win an Olympic Gold Medal in the slalom for the United States.

Ovomaltine Photo

Shirley Garms' balance is as fine as her timing. She's watching the 1-3 spot.

Thumb and index finger are pointing to the 1-3 spot as Floretta McCutcheon rolls the ball. She was able to teach a lot of future champions the art of this delivery.

Wilma Rudolph outclasses the field in the 200 meters final in the 1960 Olympic Games in Rome. Hers was called "the loosest and sweetest stride of them all."

United Press International, Inc.

Glenna Collett drives on the Homestead course at Hot Springs, Virginia. This was the scene of one of her greatest victories.

Photo by Action!

Margaret Varner's squash racquets form is stylish and precise. Note her eyes on the ball.

The power of Helen Wills Roark's game is clear in this running forehand drive.

Theresa Weld Blanchard was the first American figure skating champion and one of the greatest of all time.

ANN CURTIS CUNEO

[1926–   ]

Ann curtis was fifteen when she appeared at the Crystal Plunge in San Francisco, in 1941, and asked to join Charles Sava's swimming team. She was a gangling teenager, with more than ordinary confidence and determination. The fact that Charley Sava was one of the greatest swimming coaches in the country didn't cause her more than a moment's hesitation in presenting herself.

Ann had been bitten by the water bug when she was a student at Ursuline Convent, in Santa Rosa, California, where the sisters taught her how to swim. She had decided then that she was going to be a champion.

Charley had another opinion of Ann's swimming prospects, after she had given him a sample of her style. He confessed, later, "To me she looked like a very poor novice. I watched her stroke, then turned her down. Her mother came back afterward and begged me to take her. Ann, her mother said, was heartsick and knew deep down that she could be great. I finally put her on, but not because I expected anything . . . just because I was soft-hearted."

It was no smoothly paved road that Charley started Ann on. She swam seven days a week, three miles a day. At the end of two months, her coach realized that he had a "find," and he began to take a really serious interest in her.

Ann's perseverance and a determined chin were reliable keys to her character. She had to adjust to two unhappy events in her early childhood. She faced one with enough courage and the other with enough final understanding to keep a good sense of balance.

In the early 1930's, the Curtises were burned out of their Mill Valley home, across the bay from San Francisco, by a fire that swept over and devastated much of that part of northern California. Not long afterward, her parents, Florence and Marvin Curtis, Jr., were divorced. Her father later became a hero as a Captain in the Marine Corps during World War II, was seriously wounded at Guadalcanal and died of a heart attack at forty-two, after his discharge because of spinal injuries.

It wasn't until Ann was a famous champion, some years later, and helped dedicate the Mill Valley Tennis Club's swimming pool that she learned her father was one of the founders of the club. By chance, she saw his name on the club charter. He was a fine all-round athlete in his youth, and it may be that Ann inherited her athletic prowess from him.

After the divorce, Mrs. Curtis took her children to Fresno and Santa Rosa and, finally, back to San Francisco where Ann had been born on March 6, 1926.

Ann was seventeen when she entered her first national championship, in Shakamak Park, Indiana. She won the 440 and 880 yard free style, set a record and was high point scorer, as she was to be in eleven consecutive national meets, indoor and outdoor. No one has succeeded in breaking this record, although her times have now been lowered.

The power, rhythm and timing of her stroke had been developed to such a fine point by Charley Sava and her own hard work that Ann began to win with undeviating regularity. She took the outdoors 100-yard free style, 1944–1948; the 440, 1943–1948; the 880, 1943–1948; the mile in 1944 and 1946. Her indoor record was almost as impressive: the 100-yard free style in 1945 and 1947; the 220, 1944–1948; the 440, 1944–1948. In 1944, she was selected for the Helms North American World Trophy.

When Ann had graduated from Washington and Gallileo High School, in San Francisco, she entered the University of California, at Berkeley. She had intended to major in physical education, but changed it to philosophy and public speaking. It wasn't long before the weekday commuting to college from San Francisco, working out in the pool twice a day, and doing most of her studying on street cars and trains began to wear her out. Her swimming wasn't improving fast enough to suit coach Sava, who had the coming big meets in view. He urged Ann to drop out of college, and she did, in 1945.

World War II brought many requests from service camps throughout the country for exhibitions by the Crystal Plunge team, and Ann was one of the swimmers most in demand. But she was more than just a superb swimmer, delighting experts and novices alike with her artistry. This fact was high-lighted in 1947 when she was presented with the Sullivan award—the only swimmer to receive it, to date. The award, named for the great fighter John L. Sullivan, is presented annually by the Amateur Athletic Union to "the amateur athlete who, by performance, example and good influence did the most to advance the cause of good sportsmanship during the year."

In this same year, Ann became the first American woman to swim 100 yards in less than one minute (59.4 seconds)—a world record. This was indeed a year of triumph for her.

Ann returned to the University of California in 1948, but it seemed to her that she had hardly entered again when she had to go to Florida for two weeks for the Nationals; take two more days filming Olympic advance movies for MGM-20th Century Fox; then off to Hawaii for a tune-up meet. By the time she returned to Berkeley, she was so far behind in her studies that she had to drop out again—this time for good. She was sad that she couldn't continue and get a degree, but the choice—swimming or college, had to be made. She knew that there would be many advantages in the opportunity to travel and meet interesting people all over the world as a champion swimmer, so she didn't feel that her choice was unwise.

During World War II, the Olympics, of course, had not been carried on, so Ann set her goal for the 1948 Games, to be held in London, in August. By this time, she had accumulated four world's records, 25 national championships and several French and Hawaiian records.

From the moment Ann entered the water to swim for the Olympic title in the 400 meters free style, there seemed little doubt that she would win. There was driving power in her rhythmic action, expert timing in every stroke that left the competition behind.

After this victory, she came within two-tenths of a second of winning the 100 meters free style from Miss G.M. Anderson of Denmark.

Then came her greatest triumph, when she anchored the relay team. The Americans were third, going into the final 100 meters. Ann picked up ten yards to win—an incredible feat. The report of the United States Olympic Committee on the 1948 games summed up her record:

"Ann Curtis, United States aquatic great, took the 100 meters title and also anchored the relay team to victory in a new Olympic record time of 4:29.2. Her relay stint was hailed by many as the outstanding individual achievement of the entire Olympiad."

With two gold medals, one silver medal and other mementos of the 1948 Olympics, Ann decided to retire from amateur competition. She had worked and trained hard for eleven years. All Northern California and, San Francisco, particularly, gave her a rousing reception on her return from England. San Francisco put on a ticker-tape parade for her that was one of the most enthusiastic ever seen in a city well-known for its appreciation of its champions. During the ceremonies that followed, she was presented with the key to the city, and the keys to a new convertible automobile, as further evidence of the citizens' admiration and affection for their "home town girl."

Professional offers began to pour in to Ann. She joined a sports show and toured the country. On one occasion, she was asked to swim against a seal. She thought this was undignified, and did it much against her wishes. Since a seal can swim at a speed of fifty- to sixty-miles-an-hour, the stunt was a stupid one and was dropped after a week.

Two more professional engagements, and appearances in the 1953 and 1956 Aqua Follies ended Ann's career in that field. But she went on to another valuable career. On May 29, 1949, Ann Curtis had married Gordon Cuneo, a college basketball star and a classmate of hers when she was at the University of California. In 1958, the Cuneos inaugurated the Ann Curtis Swimming Club. Their children Bill, eight, Carrie, six, and Susie, three, at the time, would have seemed enough to keep Ann occupied, but she gave as much as fourteen hours a day to teaching other young swimmers, as well as keeping the family members of the club happy. A son, David, was born the year after the swimming club was opened. All but he are competitive swimmers and medal winners on the Ann Curtis Swimming Club's junior team. Perhaps, in time, David will be, too.

Gordon Cuneo takes great pride in Ann's swimming school. Although he is sales manager for General Motors Acceptance Corporation in the area, he found time on week nights, weekends and vacations to do nearly all the construction and landscaping of their club facilities himself.

Today, the club plant is valued in excess of $100,000. It has two pools and an underwater window from which Ann and her staff can study the swimming form of her pupils and correct any mistakes.

Ann teaches, coaches her speed team of thirty members, answers the phone, makes change for the "goodies" dispenser and finds time to answer the innumerable questions that come her way.

She is another of those great champions who has benefitted very much personally from her sport and who is determined to try to give back as much as she has received.

MILDRED (BABE) DIDRIKSON ZAHARIAS

[1914–1956]

To WRITE about Babe Didrikson is to tell a story of the woman who was voted "Greatest Female Athlete of the Half Century" by the Associated Press, in 1949. It is difficult to decide in which field of sport to place her when you have to choose one. She excelled in all track and field events. In basketball, she was named on the All-America Women's team three times. She has been called the greatest woman golfer of all time. There is little doubt that, had she wanted to, she could have become a champion at swimming, diving, tennis, billiards, lacrosse and bowling.

Her baseball throwing record is still on the books, and she could hit almost as well as she pitched. She kicked a football like a man, as she played every other game she entered; and she even considered boxing. Although she could throw a powerful straight punch, she decided against the ring, which was fortunate for the golfing world—excluding, of course, most of her opponents!

In the fall of 1944, Babe and I took part in a roundtable broadcast about our experiences in our fields of sport. Mine was limited to tennis, on this occasion. Babe had experiences in many sports to talk about, and her stories were so interesting and amusing—one following another in rapid succession—that the hour of broadcasting time hardly seemed to have begun before it was over.

This was the first time I had met her. I had known many champions in my day, and I had learned how to recognize them from the "also rans." One look at her made it clear to me why she was the greatest. Part of her unmistakable quality was to be read in her gray-green eyes and the set of her jaw. I believed then that she would be able to win a championship in any sport she wished to master. I didn't realize at the time that what I thought of her had already been written by all the experts in all the sports that interested her.

You have to go back to the Babe's teens for her first remarkable record. To those who knew her when she was growing up in Beaumont, Texas, the record couldn't have been very surprising. Perhaps even those who knew her in Port Arthur, Texas, where she was born (her family moved from there when she was three and a half years old) wouldn't have been surprised, for she was a sturdy and precocious child, showing signs of unbeatable determination in every action, even at that very early age.

Anything children did in the way of outdoor games, Babe did better. She went a step further when she won a prize at the Texas State Fair for a dress she made in grade school.

She wanted to be best in everything—and she was in everything at which she was determined to succeed.

In 1932, when she had just turned eighteen, the Employers Casualty Company of Dallas, Texas, whose officials had given her a job in 1930 because they wanted her on their basketball team, sent Babe to the National Women's AAU Track and

Field championships and Olympic tryouts at Dycke Stadium, the Northwestern University field near Evanston, Illinois. She went as a one-woman team. Of the ten individual events for which she was eligible, she was entered in eight, including the shot put and discus throw, both of which she had hardly tried before this meet. She won five events, tied for first in a sixth, scored a total of thirty points and won the meet single-handed.

George Kirksey, covering the meet for the United Press, called it "the most amazing series of performances ever accomplished by any individual, male or female, in track and field history." Later, Paul Gallico, an old friend of Babe's, wrote, "I cannot think of any male athlete with the possible exception of old Jim Thorpe who had come even close to spread-eagling a track meet all by himself."

With this triumph behind her, Babe went on to the Olympic Games in Los Angeles, two weeks later, where she competed against the top women athletes of every nation. There were only five individual track and field events for women on the program, but she entered three of them—the limit for one person. They were the javelin throw, the hurdles and the high jump. She set a world record in both the javelin throw and the 80-meter hurdles, and was ready for the high jump. This turned into a contest between Babe and Jean Shiley. Both broke the world record height of five feet, five inches. The bar was moved up another three-quarters of an inch for the tie jump-off. Jean Shiley just missed getting across. Babe took her turn and soared over the bar with several inches beneath her. But she did it with a Western roll, kicking up and over. As she hit the sawdust on the ground, the bar came down. There was another jump-off. The bar was lowered to five feet five and a quarter inches, to give Babe and Jean a chance to break their first-place tie.

Jean went cleanly over the bar. So did Babe. But the judges disallowed Babe's jump, ruling that she had dived and that her head had gone over before her feet. The Western roll is legal today, but, even then, a picture of her jump shows her feet going over the bar just before her head. Babe was certain enough that this was so, to feel that she should express her opinion about it to the judges. They answered, "If you were diving before, we didn't see it. We just saw it this time." This was small consolation to Babe. It cost her a clean sweep of the Olympic events she had entered.

The loss of this one event really mattered little when it came to establishing Babe Didrikson firmly as the greatest woman athlete in her own country, and it might well have been in the world. Many experts, foreseeing her future, called her the greatest woman athlete of all time.

Something important happened to Babe immediately following her final Olympic performance. Grantland Rice, who had been covering the Games, talked to her after the high jump event. He thought she had been given a bad deal, as many of the other sports writers did. "Granny," as he was affectionately known, liked her as much as he admired her, so he invited her to play golf with him and some friends at the Brentwood Country Club, near Los Angeles. She didn't know, when the invitation was extended, that the friends were Paul Gallico, Westbrook Pegler and Braven Dyer. "Granny" Rice took Babe as his partner, and they won.

This was the beginning of her dedication to the game that was to bring her the greatest fame of her athletic career.

When Babe made up her mind to be a golf champion, she set a standard of practice for herself that ought to be "must reading" for every aspiring athlete.

In 1935, she was aiming at the Texas state women's golf

championship. She had been medalist in her first tournament, the Fort Worth Women's Invitational. This was a feat incredible enough for the Texas newspapers to blazon in banner headlines: "Wonder Girl Makes Her Debut in Tournament Golf; Turns in 77 Score." She was eliminated in an early round of the match play that followed, but she had satisfied herself that, with intensive practice and the experience the Fort Worth tournament had given her, she could reach her goal.

On weekends, she practiced twelve and sixteen hours a day. During the week, when she was working at Employers Casualty, who had given her job back to her, she got up at the "crack of dawn" and practiced from 5:40 until 8:30. On her lunch hour, she practiced putting in her boss's office because it was the only one that had a carpet. She chipped balls into his leather chair. When her workday was over at 3:30, with the consent of her employer, she went out on the golf course, where George Aulbach gave her an hour's instruction. Then she practiced all the shots in the game for so long that she got blisters on her hands. She taped the blisters and, before she was through practicing, there was blood all over the tape. When her day was finally over, because it was too dark to practice any more, Babe went back to the room she had rented in Dallas, had her dinner, then went to bed and read the golf rule book that she came to know as well as those who wrote it.

On the fourteenth of May, 1935, the United States Golf Association ruled that Babe was a professional because she had played as a professional in other sports. By a similar ruling, the United States Lawn Tennis Association declared her a professional after she had devoted so many hours to this game that she became expert enough to consider entering major competition. She was labeled as a professional before she had even put in her entry for a tournament! This made about as much sense as taking back all of Jim Thorpe's 1912 Olympic medals because he had played semi-pro baseball on a hotel team when he was in college, a practice that was prevalent at that time to make a little money in summer time for college expenses. Most of the sports writers of long experience and importance deplored the decision on Babe's status as they did on Jim Thorpe's.

In 1938 Babe married George Zaharias, a wrestling champion of Greek descent. This was a very happy marriage. George gave Babe all the help and confidence she needed to come back to her world of golf and to win, after an absence of three years during which time she regained her amateur status by not competing in any professional events. By 1947, she had set a record of fifteen straight tournament victories. Now she intended to win the British Women's Amateur championship. If she did, she would be the first American woman to win it.

Her path was not an easy one as she went on her way to the final at Gullane, on the Scottish seashore where the championship was played. During the tournament, a woman Babe had seen following her rounds on the golf course invited her to tea. Babe always wanted to make friends with everyone, so she accepted. They had just settled down for their tea in the clubhouse when the woman asked her guest if she wasn't worried about the jinx against American players in the British Amateur, citing the failure of Glenna Collett and Virginia Van Wie to win the tournament. Babe's answer was characteristic. "I didn't come over here to lose." That didn't seem to discourage the woman, for every time she saw Babe at the hotel or in the club she would remind her, "Don't forget about the jinx."

Nothing was further from Babe's worries. When she was on the golf course she played golf, and nothing could distract her from her determination to win.

A crowd of over 5000 people saw Babe win the British title from the Scottish champion, Jean Donald, seven and five—a runaway score in an eighteen hole match.

In 1953, Babe faced her toughest opponent—cancer. It was the only thing that she couldn't beat, in the final reckoning. She had done a tremendous amount, through the American Cancer Society and the Damon Runyan Foundation, toward helping people who suffered from this disease. Later, she was to open the Babe Didrikson Zaharias chapter of the American Cancer Society in Seattle, which was created in her honor, and to give unstintingly of her time in personal appearances and radio and television spots for the cause of cancer research. Wherever she played in golf tournaments, she would visit cancer patients and try to raise their spirits. She did, by her own example.

About three and a half months after an operation which required difficult adjustment Babe entered the Tam o' Shanter "All American" at the Tam o' Shanter Country Club in Niles, Illinois. She hit her opening drive 250 yards and the spectators screamed as if they were at a football game. This was a part of her answer to the golfing public's question of which she was well aware: "Is Babe still capable of tournament golf?" To Babe, finishing among the leaders didn't represent her goal in tournament play. Winning was what she always had, and always would, set out to do. She lost out in the end, placing third, but her performance brought her many inspiring letters, particularly from cancer sufferers.

She went on playing and won the Sarasota Open and the Babe Didrikson Open in Beaumont, Texas, and was also awarded the Ben Hogan Trophy for the Greatest Comeback of the Year. The following year, she won the National Open, the All-American Open and the Vare trophy. In 1955, she won the Tampa Open and the Serbin Diamond Golf Ball in Miami Beach; but she was only able to tie for seventh place in the Augusta Titleholders. She had great pain in her back during many of her matches and was forced to return to the hospital. A month later, the doctors found a new trace of cancer. X-ray treatment was started, and the doctors said it would be three to six months before she could play tournament golf again. Her reaction to this news was once more characteristic: "As far as I was concerned, there was no doubt about my coming back again. With the love and support of the many friends I have made, how could I miss? . . . Winning has always meant much to me, but winning friends has meant the most."

In 1956, Babe died of cancer. The sporting world, in particular, and the world in general, as well, were saddened that the life and career of the gallant Babe Didrikson Zaharias had come to an end. But she left a priceless legacy to anyone who wants to be a winner in any way: the story of her life.

GRETCHEN KUNIGK FRASER

[1919–   ]

GRETCHEN FRASER came down the slope at breakneck pace, cutting a winding swathe in the snow. As she executed a sharp turn, a white spray flew up beside her. Her action was beautiful to see, frightening when one imagined the skill, timing and sheer stamina demanded of a human being to make this really perilous journey to a championship on two pieces of waxed wood.

The year was 1940. Gretchen was skiing from the top of Mt. Baldy to the bottom, at Sun Valley, Idaho in the first Diamond Sun time test run. At the end of the course, she became the first person to win this event. She repeated the feat in 1941.

Gretchen was probably born to skiing. Her mother, Norwegian by birth, skied as a child on her native slopes, and when she married and went to Tacoma, Washington, to live, she encouraged the development of skiing on Mt. Ranier. It was in Tacoma that Gretchen Kunigk was born February 1, 1919 and brought up. Here, she had her start at skiing when she was sixteen.

Don Fraser had just returned from Europe in 1937 when Gretchen met him. He had been a member of the 1936 United States Olympic Ski team. They fell in love, were married in

October, 1939, and went to Sun Valley to live. It was here that Gretchen had her first chance at real training, and the opportunity to ski every day.

The following year, she and Don were chosen for the Olympic Ski team, but the Games were canceled because of World War II. This didn't interrupt Gretchen's procession of victories. In 1941, she added the National Combined and Women's Downhill (Open) championships to the Diamond Sun, and, in 1942, the National Slalom, Harriman Cup and Silver Belt.

When Don joined the Navy to serve for four years, there was no skiing for him and little for Gretchen. The year he was overseas, she taught skiing, riding and swimming to amputees in Army hospitals, and was a great favorite among all the men to whom she gave hope of activity in spite of their disabilities.

After the war was over, Gretchen and Don started the Don Fraser Company in Vancouver. It was a small gasoline and oil distributing company. Don was the driver and Gretchen the bookkeeper. Their business thrived, so there was little time for skiing, but Don encouraged Gretchen to try out in 1947 for a place on the 1948 Olympic team. In spite of lack of practice, she won the tryouts at Sun Valley.

When she arrived with the team in St. Moritz, Switzerland, where the Winter Games were to be held, some of the foreign press described her as an unknown from America—an odd and surprising description to her and her teammates who knew her winning record. But Gretchen is blessed with one champion's quality in particular—tremendous emotional and nervous control. The patronizing press had no effect on her confidence.

The combined Downhill and Slalom preceded the race that Gretchen really had her heart set on winning—the Special Slalom. It comprised 39 gates. She was second to the winning Austrian skier, Erika Mahringer, in the Slalom, but she was so

far ahead of her competitors in the Downhill that she was only
one-tenth of a point behind first place in the Combined. The
silver medal she won made her the first American skiing victor
in the 1948 Olympic Games.

Then came the Special Slalom. Gretchen drew the number
one position—a tough assignment that puts a particular strain
on any racer. He has no opportunity to compare his performance with those of his competitors, while they can watch him
run and the mark he sets gives them all a goal at which they can
shoot. Gretchen skied the first Slalom in the faultless time of
59.7. One skier after another, experts in the field, failed by
split seconds to reach her mark. It was a thrilling race, and a
quick tabulation of results showed that four skiers were within
one and one-tenth seconds of Gretchen Fraser's winning time.

The course was in excellent condition, so it was unnecessary
to change it for the second Slalom.

The spectators watched the competitors climb slowly up the
long, steep slope for the final run to decide the Gold Medal. At
the top of the slope, Gretchen stood ready to break the cord
that started the timing. Then an unpredictable thing happened.
The telephone from the top of the run to the bottom failed. For
eighteen minutes Gretchen stood there, waiting for the countdown. "This was very hard on already taut nerves," she remembers. Observers felt that it was probably one of the greatest nerve strains to which a racer had ever been subjected. She
had to keep clearly in mind, during the delay, the arrangement
of the groups of gates, and how fast to go to reach each one at
the right speed.

The other skiers, waiting behind Gretchen for their time to
go, had no problem. Since she had won the first Slalom, they
had nothing to lose and everything to gain.

When Gretchen finally got the countdown, 5–4–3–2–1–

GO, she pushed out of the gate so hard that she came too close for comfort at the fourth gate. But at the end of the run, she was sure she had done her best. She had only to wait for the final results to know how good her best had been.

Antoinette Meyer followed her in a flawless run, half a second quicker than Gretchen, but not fast enough to retrieve her slower first run. Georgette Thiolliere was next. Her fast, clipped style was exciting to watch, but she was three-tenths of a second slower than Gretchen's time. A row of girls followed. They were all great skiers, but they were not likely to challenge Gretchen very seriously. Lucien Schmidt-Goullet, who had been four-tenths of a second behind Gretchen in the first run, started down the course in the second run with incredible speed, but on a tricky pair of gates she caught the tip of a ski and spread-eagled between the flags. She was out of the race and Gretchen Fraser had won the Gold Medal. Her victory ride back to St. Moritz from the Slalom hill was a highlight of her victorious day.

During her stay in this old Swiss mountain town, a neighboring farmer and his wife had invited Gretchen to their cottage many times for hot bread and milk. She had accepted, and when she visited them in the mornings, she had often shared her sugar lumps with the farmer's pony. Although she spoke no French, and they no English, the three became friends, and it was the delighted farmer who furnished the open sleigh that took the American winner through the pine woods to St. Moritz on her victory ride, followed and welcomed by cheering crowds. This gesture of friendship and the kind, earnest congratulations from many other teams and from her friends were almost as thrilling to Gretchen as winning.

By the time she arrived at her hotel, flowers, gifts and telegrams were beginning to pour in. There had never been a more popular Olympic skiing victory. Everyone agreed that it had been no "flash in the pan." It takes a skier of exceptional skill to win a silver medal in the Combined and a Gold Medal in the Special Slalom. Even more, the skill must be supplemented by nerve control capable of coping with any situation that arises in a hazardous sport. C759283

To Gretchen, the greatest thrill of all was standing on the winner's platform for the presentation of the Gold Medal while the American flag was raised and the national anthem was played, for hers had not been just a personal victory.

Undoubtedly, one of the most outstanding features of Gretchen Fraser's career is her versatility. Although she is best known for skiing, her list of other interests and accomplishments is most impressive. In addition to serving as a member of the United States Ski Association and the United States Olympic Ski Association for many years, she was a director of the United States Equestrian team and is, herself, an excellent horsewoman.

For many years, she has also been a member of the 99'ers, an international women's flying organization. Gretchen started flying in 1943, but it has been in the last ten years that she has built up her rating and her flying time. She flies a twin-engine Cessna, and has single, multiengine, seaplane and instrument rating—all as a result of having logged some 1500 hours as pilot in command.

On October 6, 1962, Gretchen Fraser flew her Cessna from Vancouver to San Francisco, solo, on instruments. Three days later, she intended to return home but heavy icing forced her to leave the plane in San Francisco and go back by commercial plane. On October 15, a hurricane struck Vancouver and demolished the hangar where her plane was usually kept with fifteen others. All those fifteen planes were destroyed.

In 1949, Gretchen and Don Fraser had a son, Donald, Jr. This teenager is a sportsman, like his parents. He often goes with them on shooting trips—another facet of Gretchen's varied activities. The Frasers train their own dogs for field and upland bird shooting. One, a Labrador retriever, was given to Gretchen when she won the Olympics by Undersecretary of State Averell Harriman, a friend of hers and a distinguished breeder of Labradors.

Fishing is also on the Frasers' agenda. They have a small seaplane which transports them swiftly and comfortably to Canadian lakes.

In addition to being the first American to win a skiing event in the 1948 Olympics, Gretchen can lay claim to another "first." In June, 1958 she and Don spent two weeks on the Juneau Ice Cap in Alaska skiing in a TV movie called "High Adventure with Lowell Thomas." She was the first woman to live on the ice cap.

Gretchen has a strong sense of civic responsibility. She has been a volunteer worker in the therapeutic pool of the Rehabilitation Institute of Oregon for eleven years, and on the Board of the Institute for six years. She is co-chairman of the United Fund in her area and is a member of the Board of Psychological Services Clinic of the University of Portland and of the Board of the Junior League of Portland.

In her effort to contribute to sport, which has given her so much, Gretchen is unsparing of her time. In April, 1963, as a former director of the United States Olympic Ski team, she helped, in an advisory capacity, with the finish of team tryouts at the Nationals in Alaska; and as a former director of the United States Equestrian team, she assisted in getting the members on their way to the Pan American Games in Brazil, that same year.

Gretchen Kunigk Fraser has well repaid any debt she owes to the world of sport. In fact, it would seem as if sport may be still in her debt.

SHIRLEY RUDOLPH GARMS

[1924-   ]

Wʜᴇɴ sʜɪʀʟᴇʏ ʀᴜᴅᴏʟᴘʜ was in high school in 1942, bowling was a part of the physical education program. Students
who bowled two games one afternoon a week got credits for
the course. It was a pleasant way to secure them, and Shirley
participated, but she wasn't really interested in the sport that
was to bring her fame and financial security later on until her
mother, father and two brothers, George and Billy, joined her
in a family bowling league when she was nineteen. The competition was exciting, but more important to her was the fun
of the family association.

Shirley showed promise of becoming a winner at bowling
from the moment she began to take the game seriously. Timing, grace and the determination to learn—all the ingredients
for success were there. When the family bowled at Des Plaines
Bowling Lanes, in Des Plaines, Illinois, where Shirley was born
on January 18, 1924, the manager, E.M. Kennedy, noticed her
natural co-ordination and offered to help her develop the fine
points of the game. She accepted eagerly. Her father and
mother added what they could to his instruction and in 1944
encouraged her to set a trio of goals for herself—the All-Star,
the World's Invitational and "Woman Bowler of the Year"

title. Such heights seemed a long way off, but she was willing to work.

The next year, 1945, the goal didn't seem quite so distant when she won the Northern Illinois singles championship, and followed up with doubles victories in the Central Illinois and Indianapolis *Star* championships.

In May, 1946, Shirley married Melvin Garms. His own knowledge of bowling made him better than average at the sport, and he was a competent critic of his wife's game. In addition, he made her see the importance of a heavy practicing schedule, but it took him a little time to accomplish that. Shirley had always felt that a practice session once or twice a week was enough before a big tournament. He thought it should be several games every day.

Shirley's first big test was the Chicago Match Game championship for the 1951–1952 season, to be held in October. The other tournaments in which she had participated had been nine games, and were usually bowled in one or two days. It was easy to keep in form for such a short time. But it was a different matter to bowl twenty-four games over a two or three week period and stay sharp. Shirley stayed sharp, with Mel's help, and came out of the competition triumphant over a tough field. Her confidence mounted. This year, for the first time, she became a Bowling Proprietor's Athletic Association All-Star finalist, placing fifteenth.

Mel Garms had won his argument. Shirley had set a rigorous schedule for herself, bowling about fifty games a week. Sometimes, in these early days of her career, she would spend money for bowling and do without something she really needed. But she would do it again without regrets.

Her first big win in Chicago was one of a record six. She won again from the 1953–1954 to the 1961–1962 seasons. Along the way, she picked up regional championships in team, doubles and all-events and became the undisputed "Queen of Chicago Bowlers." In the 1960–1961 season, she reached one of her major goals. She was named "Woman Bowler of the Year" by the Bowling Writers Association of America. She had won the Professional Women's Bowling Association North American championship and eight comparatively minor titles.

Mel Garms had detected a slight fault in his wife's delivery in the autumn of 1960. She was pulling her arm across her body, instead of following through with the pendulum swing. She was also "breaking" her wrist on the pushaway, instead of keeping it firm. When she corrected these faults, she got much more roll on the ball, which meant high scores with less effort.

In 1961, the World's Invitational Match Game championship opened in November, at McCormick Place. This was a splendid new exhibition hall on the Lake Michigan shore that was a welcome relief to the contestants from the dismal old Coliseum where the four previous tournaments had been held. Most of the experts named the defending champion, Marion Ladewig of Grand Rapids, Michigan, who had won the title twice, as a certain winner, for, in spite of Shirley Garms's title as "Woman Bowler of the Year" for the previous season, Mrs. Ladewig had an impressive array of titles. She had won the BPAA All Star tournament seven times, and had been named "Woman Bowler of the Year" from 1950 through 1959. But Shirley had been moving steadily up in the World's Invitational. She was twenty-first in 1957, eleventh in each of the two following years and fifth in 1960.

More important, Shirley had acquired the champion's experience and was prepared mentally, physically and emotionally to bowl for the title she had wanted for so long. Before this, she had felt that she didn't deserve to be a champion because she hadn't given enough of herself to the game. Many of those who knew her well thought she was "too nice" to develop the "killer instinct"—a quality of outstanding champions. But a friend, Olga Gloor, thought otherwise. Mrs. Gloor had won the 1959 World's Invitational, interrupting Marion Ladewig's reign. She thought the bowling public was going to see a new Shirley Garms, and that she was the big threat in the tournament; that Shirley had learned not to defeat herself by tensing up in her eagerness to win. Mrs. Gloor said, in an interview at the time, "She knows what to do in the clutch. At the Women's Professional in Cleveland last August, Shirley had three girls breathing down on her after the next-to-last game, but she kept pouring in the strikes to win the title pretty easily. That, to me, is the 'killer instinct.' " In the sports world, this is a term designating the highest admiration.

Mrs. Gloor's opinion was reinforced the month before the World's Invitational, in the finals of the Chicago City Match Game tournament. At the beginning of the last two-game round, Shirley had a very slight lead over the defending champion, Joy Abel. Then, in the position round, she opened with a 255 game for her sixth Chicago City victory.

Shirley was well aware that she had "choked up" in the pinch in former years. She admitted, "I remember when I first started making the finals of the big tournaments I would go up to the standing board, look at the names and wonder to myself, 'What am I doing here?' But I always seemed to bowl well against the bigger name bowlers."

This may be so because, as her friends say, "She doesn't know a stranger, and is one of the friendliest bowlers ever to step up on a bowling approach." This very fact presents her opponents with a difficult situation: they enjoy bowling against her because she makes them enjoy the game and roll good

41

scores; but she is so nice that they don't like to beat her.

A story is told of Pat Sachs of Houston, who was entered in her first All-Star finals at San Bernardino, California, in January, 1961, and had to bowl against Shirley. She beat her twice and burst into tears because she had forced her charming adversary into the difficult task of having to win twice in the position round to take the title, which she failed to do.

Shirley admits that she would rather have friends than be a champion, "if being a champion means not talking to my opponents. I have as much desire and determination as anyone. I just don't show it like some. By not showing a temper when I miss a spare, some people think I don't care. Inside, I'm hurting just as bad as anyone."

It took more than determination not to beat herself to bring Shirley Garms to the point of physical fitness she achieved in 1961. The year before, she had started on a diet to lose twenty-five pounds. The brown-haired, hazel-eyed champion is five feet eight inches tall and strong-boned, so she thought 165 pounds wasn't too much weight until her doctor said to her, "Shirley, you look like you're getting broad across the beam." He put her on a strict calorie diet, she went down to 140 pounds—and her scores began to go up. In the Milwaukee Friendly Ladies' tournament in February, 1961, she broke the women's world all-events record with an amazing 2022 total. Her rhythm and approach had improved, and she was reaching out more and bending from the knees instead of the waist. Now, if her weight goes up as much as three pounds, she takes it off right away.

Shirley came into the 1961 World's Invitational prepared temperamentally and physically to win. But this wasn't to be her year. The winner was Margaret "Marge" Merrick of Columbus, Ohio, who has been a finalist four times in the World's

Invitational tournaments, finalist eight times in the BPAA All-Star tournaments, Detroit's "Queen of Bowling" from 1957–1960 and in 1962 was selected for the 1962 *Bowling Illustrated* All American Team. Her victory cast no shadow on either Shirley Garms or Marion Ladewig, who was also a contestant. They had lost to a very worthy opponent.

As disappointing as her defeat was, it didn't discourage her or block her path for long. In January, 1962, playing in the BPAA All-Star tournament, in Miami Beach, Florida, she reached the final three-game block on top. Previously, in bowling the last round—a position round—a player carried any lead she had accumulated into this block. But the format was changed this year, and the first and second finishers bowled three games with total pin-fall deciding the winner. She bowled against her fellow Chicagoan, Joy Abel, and after rolling games of 231 and 202, found herself 47 pins behind with one game to go. Joy had scored 256 and 224. They started the last game. After four frames, Shirley was 54 pins behind in totals. In the 5th and 6th frames she got two good pocket hits, but in the 7th frame she over-turned the ball slightly and it crossed the head pin, missing the 1-3 pocket goal. She said a prayer for that one. Ten pins fell for a strike! She followed with two more strikes, while Joy was running into trouble with splits. A check of the score sheet showed that all Shirley needed was a good count and a spare to win in the 10th frame. She got the spare, struck on the extra ball, and won by nine pins. Another goal had been reached. She had won the All-Star, and she has never forgotten the 7th frame crossover strike that secured the title for her.

Now, Shirley moved her goal still higher—the Triple Crown. This meant winning the BPAA singles and doubles and the team championship. No woman had ever worn this crown. Her chance came in April, 1962, at Louisville, Kentucky. But she and her teammate, Pat Senning, were defeated by five pins. This defeat detracts very little from her record as 1962's "Woman Bowler of the Year" or from the impressive record that goes with her name in any of her championship years. She has won fifty championships in twenty years of bowling. It will be difficult to better that record.

Bowling has meant a lot to Shirley Garms in many ways. Most importantly, the interest of her husband. They have been married eighteen years and, during that time, he has played a wise and important part in her rise to top championship quality. When he told her that she was the "world's laziest bowler" and added, "if you're going to bowl—bowl—otherwise give it up," she started playing five games a day, every day. Mel Garms knew what he was talking about, and Shirley knew he did.

Charlie Crovetti's "Strike 'n Spare" in Northbrook, Illinois, reserves two lanes every day for Shirley. This is her home establishment, and is only about five minutes from Glenview Naval Homes, Inc., where she is housing manager at the private home project for military personnel. Mel is maintenance manager of the complex. Charlie arranges that one lane will be slow and one fast, so she will be prepared for either condition of lanes in a tournament. This is important, for a slow lane takes a hook, whereas a slick, fast lane does not let the ball break very much, and the bowler has to turn the ball when he rolls, in order to make it hook.

There isn't much her friends and fans wouldn't do for Shirley Garms. No athlete has ever had a more devoted or confident following. They know that more is yet to come from her.

CAROL HEISS JENKINS

[1940-   ]

THE FIGURE SKATING CLUB of Brooklyn was giving an exciting ice show one evening in 1944. The stands were jammed as the performers glided onto the rink, and when they went into their intricate leaps and spins, a thunder of applause followed them. Then there was a pause in the skating and silence in the gallery as a great box was carried onto the ice. The skaters circled around it, and the spectators leaned forward, staring at it curiously.

Suddenly, the box was opened, and out jumped a blonde four-year-old girl in a pretty skating costume. Scarcely hesitating when she touched the ice, she began to waltz around the rink like a little doll, with curls flying. The crowd roared. This was Carol Heiss's first public appearance in a sport that was to bring her world fame and, more important to her, her parents' dream come true.

From the day she was born in Ozone Park, Long Island, on January 20, 1940, Edward and Marie Heiss felt that theirs was no ordinary baby. She was tiny but beautifully formed. As she grew older, her energy and quickness kept her mother constantly bustling to watch over her.

She was just three and a half when Marie and Edward Heiss

45

came home from shopping one day with a tiny pair of roller skates for her. Marie had been a little reluctant to buy them. "Carol's so little!" she said to her husband. "And I would be afraid to let her skate on the sidewalk. It's too dangerous."

Edward agreed. Then he thought of a solution. "She can skate in the basement."

When they showed Carol her present, she could hardly wait for the skates to be put on. As soon as they were, in the safety of the basement, she held her father's hand and took a few tentative steps, rolling and slipping. Soon she began to find her balance and, letting go her father's hand, skated away from him.

"I can't believe it!" her mother cried.

"Only three and a half!" Her father shook his head in amazement.

Carol had been born with a sense of balance. When winter came, and her parents decided that she must have ice skating lessons, she took to the single-bladed skates with such ease at her first attempt that the instructor declared he could teach her nothing—and returned Marie's money.

Now it was important to find a more advanced teacher. Two of the best in the country, Pierre and Andrée Brunet, taught at the Junior Figure Skating Club in New York. Both had been Olympic champions in Paris. Marie took Carol to them. After watching the little girl skate, they willingly accepted her as a pupil, but it was Andrée who would teach her, for Pierre took only the most advanced skaters.

Friendship grew between the four-year-old and the Brunets, who saw in her unlimited promise. One day she announced, "When I grow up I am going to be the world's champion figure skater." They didn't in the least doubt that this was possible.

46

But there was work—hard work—ahead of Carol. Andrée was an exacting teacher. Everything must be learned to perfection, for Carol had shown more than promise. The Brunets had recognized in her the heart of a champion. "She never gives up," they said one day to her mother, who always brought her to the rink. Andrée added, "We believe that, if she studies hard, she can be champion of the world in ten years."

Carol was six now. It was difficult for her parents to believe that she could reach such a height at sixteen, but they were happy to be convinced that it was quite possible. As for Carol, she was so excited at the thought that others, who had themselves been Olympic champions, believed she would achieve her goal that she lost interest in everything but skating. Schoolwork became a chore. She missed many classes because of skating practice or appearances at shows or competitions, and it was not easy to make up the lost time.

On the rink, she was working harder than ever. There was free-skating—jumps, spins and loops of her own choosing, made to music; and there were the compulsory school figures which accounted for sixty per cent of the points in competition. Learning school figures was her most arduous task. There were 62 types, each some form of the figure 8, and they had to be performed perfectly for a top score.

Andrée worked with Carol every day on the intricate loops, brackets and counters; taught her the importance of making each tracing on the ice exactly over the previous one; and impressed upon her that the outside and inside of her skate blades made different patterns on the ice, for the judges were strict in deciding if the correct side had been used.

The day came when Carol had to take the official test given by the Skating Club. She would have to pass it if she wanted to remain a member. There were eight tests in all, including forward and backward skating, inside and outside circle, waltz and free skating.

Although she was nervous, for most of the skaters were older than she, Carol found her confidence as she went into her school figures. On she skated, light as a bird, and the judges were in a dilemma. She was *so* light that the blades scarcely cut the ice, and it was almost impossible to tell if one pattern was directly over the other. They stared at the ice and studied the figures, shaking their heads. Then, finally, they decided. She had passed.

This test marked a turning point in Carol's career. The great Pierre Brunet himself decided to take her as a pupil for the more difficult lessons that must follow, warning her that she would have to practice five to eight hours a day. She was eight years old now, and already an accomplished skater, but he wanted to push her on toward the championship of the world.

The Heisses were thrilled. They were truly a skating family. Carol's sister, Nancy, two years younger than she, and her brother, Bruce, four years younger, were taking their first skating lessons now, and the Brunets became like a second family to them. Pierre would listen to their personal troubles and give them his kind advice, but in one sphere he was their coach —rigid in discipline, exacting in performance. If they fell on the ice, they had no sympathy from him. He would just wait for them to pick themselves up and go on.

To Carol particularly, because she was so far advanced, he said, "When you enter a jump in skating, there is no backing out. Unless you have everything right, you fall flat." Carol seldom fell.

Carol and Nancy began skating together. Although Nancy was behind her sister in training, she was better at school figures. Carol loved free skating as it gave her a chance to race

48

across the ice and try jumps and spins that she had worked out for herself. Only when Coach Brunet reminded her of the importance of school figures would she settle down to them, sometimes after tearful resistance.

At these times her mother would give her an unpleasant alternative. "Take off your skates and we will go home." Marie could make good use of the mornings, which began at 5:30, when she awakened Carol and Nancy so that she could get them to the Skating Club by seven o'clock and be sure of their having a patch of ice to practice on for less than the later morning fee.

A great deal of hard-earned money was going into the children's skating lessons and equipment these days, and now Pierre suggested piano and dancing lessons for Carol—piano because she had difficulty in keeping time with music; dancing because she couldn't tell one dance step from another, and it would help her to do her free skating properly.

The family budget was being stretched to the limit. Marie Heiss had taken a job painting fabric designs to augment her husband's income as a baker. She had been bringing her work home so she could be with her children and attend to her house. Now, she was carrying it to the rink with her, and while Carol and Nancy practiced and Bruce took his first uncertain skating steps, she had one eye for her work and the other for her children.

In the summer of 1949 Carol, Nancy, Bruce and their mother went to Michigan, where the skating rinks were open all year round. They had been there a very short time when Carol came down with whooping cough. Her illness was so serious that, when her father joined the family, he immediately rushed her to a hospital, where she was put on the danger list. For a long time she lay there, growing paler and so thin that she weighed only forty-three pounds. In time, a new medicine the doctors gave her pulled her through, but it was a whole year before Carol could skate again.

When she laced on her skates for the first time after the long lay-off, she wondered if she had forgotten all that she had learned. But after a moment's hesitation at the edge of the rink, she was off in a flash of blades, turning, leaping and spinning.

Pierre Brunet thought she was better than ever. Just after her tenth birthday, he entered her and Nancy in the Middle Atlantic Ladies' Pairs championship. They were always happy skating together and easily won first place. In addition, Carol won the Junior Ladies' title.

Next came the more difficult Eastern Figure Skating competition, at Rye, New York. Here, too, Carol took the Eastern Junior Ladies' championship, and eight-year-old Nancy won the Girls' title. The newspapers called them "The Golden Kids," and they were in demand wherever there were amateur skating events.

The only thing that worried Marie and Edward Heiss was Carol's education. She was an honor student at public school, but the principal had told Marie Heiss that her daughter would not be allowed any time off for skating—that she would have to choose between school and sport.

It was out of the question to take skating away from Carol. It had become too much a part of her life. Soon her parents found a solution—the Professional Children's School, in New York City. Here she could go to classes when she was at home. When she entered competitions away from home, she could take her work with her, and mail lesson sheets back to the school. Examinations would be given to her in private, at the nearest public school, and the tests returned to Carol's school.

She would have a fine education, to which her traveling would add the value of firsthand experience. The Professional Children's School proved so successful for her that, later, Nancy, too, was sent there.

In 1953, Carol won her first American championship—the National Juniors. In the same year, another great skater, Tenley Albright, who was five years older than she, won the National Ladies' championship, overcoming polio to achieve this triumph. Both girls were to be sent to Davos, Switzerland, to represent the United States in the World's championship. Carol and her mother, who went with her, were thrilled at both the chance she would have to skate against Tenley and the opportunity to give her best performance for the United States.

Although Tenley was the favorite, the crowds in the little Alps mountain village flocked to watch thirteen-year-old Carol in her bright red and green costume.

On the day of the final, after two preliminary days of school figures, Tenley was leading. The weather was icy cold, with a strong wind sweeping out of the mountains. Two British skaters had to be assisted, half-frozen, from the rink.

Marie Heiss made sure that Carol was warmly dressed in her white-trimmed velvet outfit and when her turn came, she gave her an encouraging hug. "I know it's rough, darling, and we don't expect you to win the first time," she said. "Just do the best you can."

Carol excited the crowd to wild acclaim with her "best." During the four allotted minutes as she leapt and spun across the ice, the frigid weather was forgotten.

Then Tenley's turn came. She started gliding easily, gracefully, increasing her speed to leap and whirl with such effortless skill that the spectators were breathless. When she had finished with a spin dizzying to watch, all seven judges voted her first. It was the only time an American girl had won the title.

Carol finished fourth in a formidable field. To add to the Americans' delight, Hayes Alan Jenkins, whom Carol had met at the Brunets, and with whom she often skated in pairs competition, won the men's title.

When Carol and her mother returned to the United States, her greatest ambition was to meet Tenley again and to win. She had her first chance two weeks later, in the North American competition at Cleveland, but she was just able to place second—coming up to that position from fourth only after the free skating. It was the same story in the Nationals, at Hershey, Pennsylvania.

On January 1954, Carol suffered an injury that threatened to end her skating days. She and Nancy, who had placed second in the National Novice championship, were practicing at the rink. Carol was preparing for the World Championship, to be held in Norway the following month. At the side of the rink sat Marie Heiss, working on her designs. Pierre Brunet was instructing Carol and trying to keep his eye on Nancy at the same time. As the two girls skated backward toward each other, they decided to do a turn, bumped into one another and fell down. Neither had looked where she was going. Laughing, they started to get to their feet, but Carol couldn't stand, and when she looked down at her left white boot, she saw blood running down the side of it.

Nancy cried out, "You're hurt!" and Pierre flew across the ice to her side. "I must have cut her with my skate!" Nancy explained miserably.

"You didn't mean it. I will be all right," Carol tried to comfort her sister.

Marie was beside herself, but she tried to be calm as they rushed Carol to a nearby doctor. He gave her first aid, and told her that she would have to stay off her feet for some time.

Carol complied with his orders for a few days, but she became restless. Her mind was on the World Championship and she wanted to get back to practice.

When she was permitted to go to the rink, claiming that her leg felt fine, she intended to start easily, but halfway across the ice her injured leg buckled under her and she fell. As soon as she got home and told her parents what had happened, her father took her immediately to their own doctor. Nothing was important to him except finding out how serious the injury was.

The doctor examined Carol's leg. Then he took her father aside and broke the bad news to him. "Mr. Heiss, your daughter may never skate again." Nancy's skate had severed a tendon below the calf of Carol's left leg.

Edward Heiss was shocked, and when he told his wife what the doctor had said she knew it would break their daughter's heart.

Edward Heiss advised, wisely, "We must tell her how serious it is, but we needn't tell her that the doctor said she may never skate again. Instead, we must encourage her. Perhaps it will help."

So they told Carol exactly what her injury was, and her mother added, "You will have to work at getting over this. That is the way to face it."

Carol worked as she never had before. She didn't want to be a cripple. Tenley Albright had overcome polio, and now she skated and swam. Carol Heiss would skate again—of that she was determined. She went regularly to the doctor for treatment, and when her parents suggested any activity to her—

housework or walking to the store, she agreed readily, knowing that they intended this only for her to exercise—although there was pain to suffer as she did so.

Nancy suffered almost as much as Carol, for she blamed herself for the accident, and, unfortunately, many of the people at the skating rink whispered among themselves that they thought Nancy had done it deliberately because she was jealous of her sister. Nancy heard them and vowed she would never skate again. It wasn't until Carol insisted that they skate together, as she prepared some weeks later for the Nationals in March, that the gossip began to die down.

When the championship was held, Carol skated brilliantly, despite her leg, but again Tenley was first and she second. Although she didn't win, Carol's performance stopped the gossip for good.

In September 1954, Marie Heiss was operated on for cancer. The family had been prepared for it, but that helped little to alleviate the misery and worry at seeing the suffering in her face and the shadow that often came across her eyes. They all knew that she could not live long. But when the time came for Carol to leave for Vienna, to compete in the World's Championship, her mother insisted on going with her. In vain, Edward pleaded with his wife not to take the trip, fearing it would be too much of a strain on her.

Carol was more determined to win this title than any she had ever sought. It might be her last chance to win a first over Tenley Albright for her mother. Pierre Brunet reminded her that she was only fifteen and Tenley was twenty, but that didn't matter to her. Carol's great rival had received several professional offers, and had turned them down, explaining that she intended to finish college and become a doctor as her father had done. That meant retirement. Carol wanted to overtake

Tenley before that time came.

Worry over her mother affected her skating in the school figures. She could get no better than sixth place, but in the free skating she gave such a brilliant performance—jumping from either foot, as she had been forced to learn to do since her injury, spinning, then seeming to soar like a bird—that she had the crowd roaring.

The decision was the same old story. Tenley, with her incredible "stage loop jumps" and "three's in spirals into a camel hump" was placed first, Carol second.

In January 1956, the Winter Olympics were to be held in Cortina d'Ampezzo, Italy, and Carol was chosen for the team. She had another chance to win for her mother—this time as the youngest girl ever to skate for the United States.

In spite of a second operation in April of the year before, Marie Heiss accompanied Carol. Because she was now so ill, they took a room off to themselves, where Marie could have long, hot baths to ease her pain. She didn't want anyone to know that she was sick. Carol's teammates felt that the Heisses thought they were "too good" for the others, and their resentment reached the press. Because Marie wanted no pity for herself or for Carol, she forbade any explanation.

The ill-will seemed to subside on January 20th, when the team celebrated Carol's sixteenth birthday. This was the year the Brunets had said she would win the World's Championship. Could she win the Olympics, too?

For the first time, she finished almost even with Tenley in the school figures. Then came the free skating. Tenley skated first. She had wrenched her leg in practice, but she forced herself to stand the pain for the four minutes of her performance, and had an almost perfect score.

Winter darkness had to be pierced by the rink lights when

Carol's turn came, an hour later. The air was frigid and a cold, stiff wind blew. But Carol was skating for her mother, and such was her inspiration that her four minutes on the ice were called "the most daring program ever skated by a woman at the Olympics."

When it was over, Carol was so cold and exhausted that she went to her room before hearing the results. She didn't know that Tenley had won and she was second. Pierre Brunet was rubbing her hands, trying to bring back the circulation to her numb fingers, when a reporter came to the door and insisted that she go out to have a picture taken, kissing Tenley.

"Are you crazy!" Pierre was indignant. "This girl is half-frozen and exhausted. Get it tomorrow." He shut the door.

The next day's newspapers carried the story of a feud between the two girls. Despite the fact that they themselves denied any bitterness, and that Carol posed with Tenley for an hour the day after the competition, the story spread.

There is no doubt that it added drama to their World's Championship meeting in mid-February, at Garmish-Partenkirchen, Germany. Another story heaped tinder on the flame. The manager of the American team, knowing nothing of Marie's illness, ordered the Heisses to move into the hotel with the rest of the team. Carol refused, saying they were quite comfortable where they were. Since they were paying for their rooms themselves, he couldn't force them to move, but the papers got wind of it, and again the rumored jealousy between America's star women skaters was in the news.

By now Marie Heiss was so ill that she was only able to get to the skating events. But she had the strength to comfort Carol when Tenley drew ahead of her in the school figures. "It isn't over," she reminded her.

Carol looked at her mother's face—thin and drawn by the

tremendous, courageous struggle to put her illness in the background of her daughter's effort. The awful sadness of it in some way spurred Carol on to skate as she never had before. The New York *Herald Tribune* told a part of the story that began for Carol as snow started to fall:

Going into tonight's free program, Miss Heiss held the narrowest of leads after the completion of the school figures earlier in the day. That in itself was a terrific upset, as never before had she defeated Miss Albright in this phase of the event. Carol put on a terrific show in the final given over to the free skating. The tiny blonde skated flawlessly, and her performance featured double axels, double flips and loops. . . .

When it was over, the crowd demanded a perfect score for the performance, crying "Six, six, six!" Carol didn't know whether she had made it or not. Then the nine judges began to announce the scores. Every one gave her 5.9—as near perfect as possible. She was the World's Champion at last! And she had won her title against the top of the field—Tenley Albright!

Best of all, her mother had seen her triumph. Everything Carol had given up for this day was worthwhile. Tears of joy ran down the faces of Pierre Brunet and of her grandparents, who had come from Munich to join Marie for the final, but on her mother's face there were no tears. In her eyes, Carol saw pride and happiness, and a message: "I knew you would." Her father's telegram told her what Marie had said so clearly without speaking.

On October 30, 1956, Marie Heiss died. In a sense it was a blessing to know that she was finally free of pain. She had seen Carol win her first great championship. Somewhere, she would know of the others to follow—three National, four more World's, three North American championships all in a row, and the Olympic title in 1960.

57

It was in the Olympics at Squaw Valley, California, in 1960, that Carol reached her greatest height as an athlete. With every day's skating, she drew further ahead of her rivals, and Pierre Brunet agreed proudly with everyone that she skated like a queen.

She had prepared a program that included 20 of the 26 most difficult jumps possible in free skating. One of them, a "left and right double axel," introduced by Dick Button when he was Olympic champion, required her to take off in a spinning jump, first from one foot then the other, in rapid succession. No other girl did it.

The crowd went wild and were silent only when time came for the judging. The marks were held up. Carol had won the gold medal!

For all the joy and satisfaction her victory brought to her and her family and the Brunets, her greatest happiness was yet to come. On April 30, 1960, Carol Heiss married Hayes Alan Jenkins, her favorite skating partner, in St. Thomas Episcopal Church in New York City. She was a beautiful bride and Hayes, the 1956 Olympic skating champion, was a very handsome groom. As they stepped from the church after the ceremony, hundreds of their fans were waiting to cheer them and wish them godspeed toward their new life together.

Today, they live in Akron, Ohio where Hayes Jenkins is a lawyer with an important firm. Carol is a housewife, a movie star and a professional skater. The movies and professionalism are to serve just two purposes in her life—to help her sister and brother, Nancy and Bruce, and to save money for the special things she and her husband want.

Skating has been good to Carol, but she has given much to it in return, in the finest traditions of a great champion.

FLORETTA DOTY McCUTCHEON

[1888–   ]

In march 1927, the greatest American bowling champion, Jimmy Smith, went to Pueblo, Colorado, to give an exhibition. Among the spectators was Floretta McCutcheon, a thirty-nine-year-old mother of two children, and, herself, a determined bowler. It was the first time she had seen a champion in action during the four years she had been playing this game, and she was fascinated by the ease with which he rolled the ball. Taking a lesson from top style, she went to work to perfect her game, and by the end of the season hard work paid off. She rolled 682 in a sweepstake.

On December 17, Jimmy Smith went to Denver for another exhibition. Floretta McCutcheon was asked to bowl against him. The thought of strange alleys, and one of the outstanding bowlers in the world as an opponent scared her. She flatly refused. But her family and friends and the Denver bowling enthusiasts persisted in urging her to accept the challenge. Finally, she agreed.

The result of this match made her the most famous woman bowler in the world. She rolled the highest three-game series ever scored against Jimmy Smith in his tours—704 to 687.

"Mrs. Mac," as Floretta McCutcheon became known to

bowlers all over the country, was born in Ottumwa, Iowa, on July 22, 1888. When she was six, her mother died and her father became Floretta's close companion. He was interested in all active games, and encouraged her love of horseback riding, running races, and even her tomboy activities—pitching ball and climbing trees.

The family moved to Denver when Floretta was fourteen. In high school she was particularly interested in mathematics and made up her mind that she would go on to college and then become a math teacher. But six years later, before those plans could materialize, Floretta Doty married Robert McCutcheon. In time, she had a son and a daughter. Great sadness came to the McCutcheons when the son died just before the family moved to Pueblo, in 1921.

It was in Pueblo that Mrs. Mac first heard of bowling. The Colorado Fuel and Iron Company YMCA had alleys, but they didn't interest her. She joined gym classes at the "Y" and learned to swim and play volley ball. When they tried to interest her in bowling, she refused to play. But the "Y" had to have a women's bowling team, so they simply told her, "You're going to bowl and like it." Mrs. Mac was thirty-five now, but she bowled—and liked it.

She wasn't too good at the start. She thought that the faster she ran to the foul line, and the harder she swung the ball, the more speed she would give it and, of course, the more pins she would knock down. One afternoon, someone explained to her that she must aim for a certain point—the 1–3 pin spare. She practiced the placement and began to get more strikes and easier spares left to roll. This became one of her most valuable lessons, and one of the reasons why top-flight bowlers noticed that she hit the 1–3 pocket like the high-average men bowlers did.

The following year, the new bowling alley manager, Mr. Ward, gave her some further advice that added to her incredible accuracy. He said, "If you'd watch the spot where you start your ball instead of the pins, you'd make a wonderful bowler." In trying to follow his advice, she seemed, at first, to lose control of the direction of the ball. Then an idea to overcome this fault occurred to her. She asked the pin boy to hold one end of a cord on the 5 pin spot, and then on the 7 and 10 pin spots, to help her visualize the angles at which she should roll her ball. She was surprised to find how slight the angles were.

She had been looking at the pins because she thought she should watch the target—the 1-3 pocket. Now she didn't aim at the pocket. She put her ball down on a spot beyond the foul line where she figured it would roll into the pocket. It did, and soon she was able to put the ball on the same spot so often that high scores became automatic.

Before the famous match with Jimmy Smith, Mrs. Mac rolled twenty games in which she had eleven strikes and one spare. Then, one day, she started her last game with seven strikes in a row. "I bet I'm going to get 300," she said to herself, and, as quick as the thought, she began to tighten up. She realized then that she had always tightened up just before the possibility of a 300. So she made herself relax by rolling the next ball as though it were the first ball of a new game. She did the same thing for the next five balls and got her first 300. She rolled her second 300 in Pueblo, also, and her last eight in exhibitions throughout the United States. No woman has equaled this record.

Mrs. Mac had a goal beyond the coveted 300. She wanted to roll a 700 series. She had come close with several 690 series. Then, one night in league bowling, as she was striking out, the scorekeeper told her, "You need 9 pins for 700." She rolled and left the 8–10 for 699. Ten days later, she rolled 789 for her first 700 in a practice series. Later on in the season, she rolled 750 in league competition in one house and 723 and 701 in another.

After the Jimmy Smith match, he suggested that she give some bowling exhibitions on her way to the Women's International Bowling Congress in Detroit. She was as reluctant to do this as she had been to compete against Jimmy in that exhibition match in Denver, for she had always lived quietly at home, and his suggestion seemed like "turning my life upside down."

She took his advice, though, and found that the eagerness for instruction of the women she met was to lead to a new life for her in bowling.

The Peoria *Star* sponsored the first "Mrs. McCutcheon Bowling School," and then other newspapers took up the idea. Thousands of entries came in. Her professional instruction expanded into a regular program, in partnership with Carl J. Cain, who had managed all of Jimmy Smith's tours. From 1930 to 1940 the pair toured. Mrs. Mac taught in many cities and towns in the United States, ran bowling schools for the New York *Telegram*, St. Louis *Post Dispatch*, Chicago *Daily News* and Philadelphia *Enquirer*, instructing girls and women from eight to eighty-three. During this time, her daughter, Barbara, after her graduation from the University of Colorado in 1934, assisted her on her tours. In was quite a thrill for Mrs. Mac when Barbara rolled a 290 game and a 792 series.

In 1943, Mrs. Mac organized the Capitol Health Center in New York. She also established the women's bowling league in that organization.

During this period, she set up many records, in addition to

the famous ten perfect games. She rolled a high three-game series of 832 in Morris, Minnesota, and a high twelve-game series of 248, including a 300-game, in St. Paul. Her ten-year exhibition average was 201 for 8076 games. She won the Olympic Bowling Tournament at Los Angeles in 1932, and was named by Grantland Rice as the only woman on his "All-Time-All-Star Bowling Team." The other members were Ned Day, Hank Marino, Andy Varipapa, Joe Norris and John Koster.

Mrs. Mac's bowling career has been most important to her for two reasons: first, it enabled her to put her daughter through the University of Colorado. Second, when newspapers began sponsoring the "Mrs. McCutcheon Bowling School," the first great influx of women into bowling started.

In the autumn of 1938, Mrs. Mac stopped touring to give all her time to teaching and organizing bowling leagues and schools of instruction—the last at the Bowlium, in Chicago. Apart from her great skill, her charm, gracious manner and earnest belief in the value of bowling were largely responsible for her enormous success in this field.

She takes great pride in the accomplishments of her pupils. One, Jean Michaels, became captain of the famous James Gray team of New York, and a winner of the Women's International Bowling Congress singles sweepstakes. Another, Ann Sabolowski, rolled 768, and was one of the outstanding bowlers in the major league that Mrs. Mac organized at the Capitol Health Center.

At the time of her retirement to Pasadena, California, in January, 1954, after setting more bowling records than any other woman, Floretta McCutcheon had the added distinction of having taught some 250,000 men, women and children, from coast to coast, to bowl. Two years later, she was named

"1956 Star of Yesteryear" by the Women's International Bowling Congress, of which she is an honorary member; and the Women's Bowling Association of the Windy City, for which she served as a Director on the Board, made her a Paid-Up Life Member. She is one of fourteen women on the honor roll of the Women's International Bowling Congress—the equivalent of the American Bowling Congress Hall of Fame.

It was written of Mrs. Mac, after she was honored as a star of yesteryear: "In the whole galaxy of WIBC stars, our Mac's shines the brightest." Everyone in the bowling world would have to agree, on the record, with this tribute to a great champion.

Today, Floretta Doty McCutcheon is living the life she likes the best—devoting her time to her daughter and grandchildren.

ALICE MARBLE

[1913–   ]

WHEN ALICE MARBLE was an outstanding California junior tennis player, it would have been hard to imagine that she would ever need more than ordinary courage to get to the top of her chosen sport.

Before her brother Dan put a tennis racket in her hand at a tender age and insisted that she learn how to play the game, baseball was the love of her athletic life. The Marble family had moved from Plumas County, California, where Alice was born on September 28, 1913, to San Francisco. Here she played sandlot baseball with boys who were quick to recognize her as their equal in skill. When she wasn't playing herself, and was free from school and family chores, she was at the ball park, watching San Francisco's professional team, the Seals, practice. She intruded so often on their activities—catching a fly or a grounder—that the players couldn't help but notice her, and they decided to make her their mascot. From then on, at every chance she had, she shagged flies and took a turn at batting and pitching. The men could see that she was a natural athlete. She had the fluid swing and pitching form—easy and balanced—and she ran like a boy. All this carried over into her service and groundstrokes and her swiftness on court during her tennis days.

Dan, who, Alice says, was "a tyrant with a very soft heart," gave her the racket to wean her away from baseball and interest her in a more lady-like sport. Whatever her brother wanted her to do was important to her, partly because he had been head of the household of five Marble children since their father had died when Alice was seven, so she put her mind to tennis.

She began to play at Golden Gate Park when she was fourteen. Her mother's interest in her game was chiefly concerned with the development of her strength, health and general well-being. She never saw Alice play, although she had the pleasure of listening to many radio accounts of her daughter's triumphs.

Alice, a rather tall, slender blonde with a charming smile, had all the natural equipment to be a great player except, she has said, the competitive spirit. She had to develop that—and I can testify that she did. She had another drawback. Learning tennis on the asphalt courts at Golden Gate Park, she was influenced by the game of California's greatest player, "Little Bill" Johnston, who was "Big Bill" Tilden's perennial rival during most of the 1920's. She hit her forehand with the Western grip—a very awkward one on the grass courts of the East, where the major championships of this country are played. With the palm of the hand resting underneath, instead of behind the handle, the low sliding ball gave her trouble. Just as Billy Johnston had to do against Tilden, Alice had to keep stooping to the low shots, in order to bring the racket face flat to the ball for power when she hit. This saps endurance in a long and strenuous match.

Her service was beautifully produced, but it carried too much top-spin, and therefore bounced too high. It was an invitation to a winning point when she played opponents accustomed to grass and liking the high shot which could be hit down onto the turf and would slide away from the pursuing player.

Two people who were to be of great importance to Alice in her athletic career saw these weaknesses in her game. One was Eleanor "Teach" Tennant. The other was Harwood "Beesie" White, brother of the writer Stewart Edward White. "Teach" had a fine tennis tournament record to her credit. "Beesie" had an extraordinary know-how in the long range of stroke production and its place in tactics and strategy.

The first thing these two instructors did was to change Alice's grips on both forehand and backhand from the Western to the Eastern. On the forehand, the palm of her hand was now behind the handle; on the backhand, her thumb was across the back of the handle. They also took the exaggerated spin out of her service—and Alice was ready to go. From this time on, she was a formidable opponent.

She would have gone straight to the top except for one thing. In 1933, she won two important tournaments—the Essex County Club and the Longwood singles, both in Massachusetts. From there she went to East Hampton, Long Island, to play in the Maidstone Club tournament, the last major invitational event before the national championships at Forest Hills. It was a hot summer day—close to a record high. Alice played 108 games on this day. From ten o'clock in the morning to one in the afternoon, she played singles against Marjorie Van Ryn—a 3-set match. With Helen Wills Moody (now Mrs. Roark), she played the semifinal doubles against the strong English team of Betty Nuthall and Mary Heely. Then she was allowed an hour's respite. The temperature had risen to 104 degrees when Alice and Betty Nuthall went on court for their final match. Betty won in three sets from an exhausted opponent.

Shortly after the singles final, Alice and Helen Wills Moody played the doubles final. They lost the match. That evening, when Alice went back to her hostess' house, she fainted. The doctor, who was called immediately, attributed her collapse to sunstroke, and told her that she was not to play again for some time.

In 1934, Alice tried to play once more, as a member of the American Wightman Cup team. I was captain of the team that year. We went to Paris in May, before the Wightman Cup matches at Wimbledon, to play team matches against the French and to compete in the French championships. I realized that Alice had come back to competition too soon when she again collapsed—this time during her French-America team match against Sylvia Henrotin, at the Stade Roland Garros.

She had to be taken to the American Hospital in Neuilly, near Paris. I couldn't go with her because I was scheduled to play the match following hers. But the mother of one of our teammates, Carolin Babcock, took her to the hospital, and I hurried there as soon as I had played my match. Her doctor told me that she had wet pleurisy and shouldn't play for a long while. I cabled the United States Lawn Tennis Association, asking for permission to send Alice home, and giving them, briefly, the reason. It was not an easy thing to do, for Alice had not been told how seriously ill she was. I made arrangements with the American Embassy in Paris for someone who was going to the United States at the same time, to accompany Alice on the ocean voyage to New York.

"Teach" Tennant met her when her ship docked, took her to California and, with proper medical care and rest, got her back on her feet and able to start practicing, in spite of the fact that four medical consultants had said that she would never play tennis again.

In 1936, Alice took my American singles championship

68

from me. It required a set and a half for her to realize that my usually strong backhand, which she had been avoiding, was of no use to me on this day. The day before, in a practice match, I had fallen on a damp grass court and dislocated my right thumb. My friend, Allison Danzig, the *New York Times* eminent tennis reporter, arranged for the trainer of the New York Giants to come to Forest Hills and strap my thumb for the final match. He did a wonderful job, but Alice's shots to my backhand were too hard hit for me to take them without the support of two hands on the racket. In the third set, she concentrated on my backhand, as she should have done from the beginning. Force of habit had probably kept her hitting to my forehand until then.

We met again at Wimbledon in 1938, after Alice's defeat in the 1937 national championship, in which she lost her title to Dorothy Bundy, a very good player but one not really in her class. This defeat had convinced her that she would never win again. When she returned to California after the tournament, she heard two good friends discussing her game. Clark Gable said to Carole Lombard, "She hasn't got it." That was all Alice Marble needed to make her determined to come back and regain her title!

At Wimbledon, she defeated the French champion, Simone Mathieu, one of the greatest players in Europe, in the quarter-final, 6–2, 6–3, although Simone led 3–1 in the second set. I think that match taught Alice the value of patience, for the French player could be as maddening as Hilde Sperling with her slow, deep, high-hit shots when she found herself in trouble. Clark Gable should have seen Alice that day! Suddenly, she put on the pressure and took five straight hard-hitting games in a row for the match.

What I remember most about our semifinal in this Wimbledon were the overhead smashes Alice missed. They were the turning points in both sets. A player's greatest strength can sometimes become a weakness if he is overconfident and therefore a little careless with it at critical points in a game. When an error is made on this strong stroke, it breaks his confidence far more than an error from an admittedly weaker stroke.

Alice should have led 4–3 in our first set. She forced me to lob as she entrenched herself at the net. I didn't put up a very good lob. She was waiting for it, and, at any other time, would probably have smashed it into the stands. She took it too hastily, and hit it way over the baseline. The same thing happened when she had a point for 5–3 in the second set. This was too much for her, and I don't blame her. In an instantaneous reaction, and not out of temper, she kicked the ball into the stands, to the delight of the Center Court spectators.

Perhaps because of these errors, Alice decided to play me from the backcourt in the second set. This gave me the chance to break up her game with a variation of drive and slice and leave the volleying position unchallenged, except for one point. At 4–4, 40–30 for me, she came up. I deliberately lobbed. She smashed beyond the baseline. I think that point ended the match.

Alice had a host of friends to help her forget her disappointment at losing this match. Wisely, I think, she confined her friendships, off the court, to non-tournament tennis players. Their other interests gave her a change from the game, and kept her from becoming stale.

Whether it was a fairly early dinner party, dancing or a theater, her amusements heightened her keenness without interfering with her training that had to go on—the athlete's diet, lots of sleep; carefully planned exercise off the court, such as running, to develop only those muscles that need to be strong, yet resilient, for championship tennis.

In the off-season months, she did many more things. Swimming, except for a short while, is too relaxing and over-develops the shoulder muscles, so this fun had to wait until autumn for Alice. Horseback riding was wonderful exercise, but there was always the possibility of a "spill," so that, too, had to wait.

Alice did what most of us did. She waited until the tennis season was over to enjoy these sports and forget the training hours.

Alice regained her American championship in the final against the Australian champion, Nancye Wynne. In perhaps one of her most difficult bids for the title, she had to play Sarah Palfrey Fabyan to a standstill in the semifinal.

Sarah won the first set and went to 5–3, 40–15, match point, in the second before Alice began to take all the chances a great champion does at such a point. She hit with all her power, went for the lines, saved match point with a magnificent volley, and dropped only five points as she won the last four games of that set.

Sarah is a great player—a singles as well as a doubles champion—and she's a fighter. She started the third set determined to win. A finer game never came from the racket of that slight player as she fought with every weapon she had for this title. She hit her way to a 3–1 lead, and everyone thought she was very close to her first national singles crown. But Alice showed, at this point, the more than ordinary courage that had brought her to this semifinal, as it had to other final rounds since her illness.

Suddenly, Alice's guns became too heavy for Sarah and she won 5–7, 7–5, 7–5. Each player had scored 122 points, which tells the story of the match.

The final round was an anti-climax. Alice made Nancye

Wynne look like a novice.

Today, Alice is teaching tennis at the San Fernando Country Club, in Deauville, California—a club of 1500 families. It is a great satisfaction to her to pass on to "the kids and the mothers" her knowledge of the game. Before this, Alice's instructing ability was proven when she taught Maureen Connelly an adequate serve; worked with Darlene Hard on her ground strokes, which showed marked improvement; and worked for twenty weeks with Billie Jean Moffat before this young player beat the great Australian, Margaret Smith, in the first round at Wimbledon in 1962. Billie Jean reached the final at Wimbledon in 1962, where she lost to Margaret Smith; but she distinguished herself by many fine wins on her way to the final.

Before Alice decided to go back into the game to which she had brought such brilliance, she served as medical assistant to three California doctors, in the children's field. Much as she felt she was accomplishing in learning laboratory skills, she finally came to the conclusion that her place was on the court, where she could put her outstanding talent to use. It is fortunate for California tennis that she made this decision.

AILEEN RIGGIN SOULE

[1906–   ]

I F AILEEN RIGGIN hadn't been a frail child, she might have been as great a swimming champion as she was a diving champion. When she was six years old, she learned to swim in the Philippines, where her father was stationed in the Navy, and she took to the water like a native. She may have had swimming in her blood, for she was born at Newport, Rhode Island, where the Atlantic Ocean sweeps the shore.

The only strokes one learned when Aileen began to swim in 1912—and for some time to come—were the sidestroke and the breaststroke. The modern crawl, backstroke and butterfly strokes had not yet been developed.

It was not until the Riggins moved to New York, when Aileen was eleven, that she took up swimming with the determination to become a champion. The family doctor had a more serious interest in her swimming—the benefit to her health. She was quite small for her age, and not very strong, and he felt that swimming would help to build her up.

She joined the Women's Swimming Association of New York just after it was founded, in 1917. This was later to become the largest women's swimming club in the world. Its members included such eventual "greats" as Gertrude Ederle, the first woman to swim the English Channel; Helen Wainwright, United States indoor 3-foot and 10-foot springboard diving champion, and a national swimming champion as well; and Helen Meany, three times United States indoor 3-foot springboard and twice 10-foot springboard diving champion, four times United States outdoor 10-foot springboard, and five times platform diving champion, and 1928 Olympic fancy springboard diving champion.

The first coach of the W.S.A. (it was known as this) L. de B. Handley, was one of the best in the country. He was developing the crawl stroke, and his pupils were probably the first girls to use this stroke in racing competition.

The W.S.A. girls dominated the field both internationally and in the Olympics, and Aileen usually made a fourth on the relay team that won the nationals during those early years.

But she soon realized that she was "too tiny and not strong enough" to be the best swimmer, so she decided to concentrate on diving, determined to be the best in that field, as she had hoped to be in swimming. An interesting thing contributed to the achievement of her goal in diving. She was studying ballet at the Metropolitan Opera House Ballet School. It seemed quite natural to combine diving with dancing. The two had much in common—muscle control, grace, timing, and pointing the toes among other things.

Unfortunately, it was not easy in those days to find facilities for diving in New York. There were no 10-foot boards (regulation championship height) available to girls anywhere in the city. The only opportunity the girls had to practice was in the summer, at beaches and clubs. Sometimes the height would be affected by the tide, and they would have to practice when it was high, whether it was at five in the morning or five in the afternoon! They had no regular diving coach, but occasionally one of the men divers from the New York Athletic Club, or a member of a college team would give them some pointers.

Since Mr. Handley only coached swimming, and that as a hobby, the girls interested in diving were pretty much on their own. They had to practice from low 1- or 2-foot boards all during the winters.

Eventually, they found a 10-foot championship height board, in New Jersey. The water under the board was only six feet deep, however—a serious hazard. This drawback, and the hours it took to travel to and from New Jersey, limited their trips to about once a week.

All divers had a problem with boards, at that time, because they were not standardized. They varied in resilience, height and covering. (Many weren't covered at all.) Some were springy, while others were as stiff as a stationary platform, so the divers never knew what to expect when they entered a contest in a strange club or pool.

They had another problem. New York winters are not mild, and contestants became colder when diving than while swimming because of the chilly winds and the frigid intervals between turns to perform out of doors.

Aileen survived the training and the tests, in spite of the hazards and in April, 1920, at thirteen, entered her first big diving championship competition in the national 10-foot springboard at the Detroit Athletic Club. The W.S.A. had sent a relay swim team to the nationals—Gertrude Ederle, Helen Wainwright, Aileen Riggin and Helen Meany. They proved victorious. Aileen entered the diving championship because she thought it would be good experience, and was surprised and pleased to place fifth against seasoned and older competitors.

Shortly after this meet, she and her teammates read about

the Olympic Games to be held that summer in Antwerp, Belgium. They tried to get information about rules and regulations and required dives, but it was months before they had an answer to their enquiries.

This was to be the first Olympic Games in which the United States would enter a women's swimming and diving team, and also the first time that women's fancy diving from a springboard was to be included. Consequently there was no precedent to follow, and Aileen and her teammates had no idea which dives were to be selected for competition.

Finally, they received the official Olympic booklet about a month before the United States Olympic team tryouts. But it was entirely in French, and it sent them racing for a translation, to find out what dives such as "*coup pied à la lune*" might mean. They found that it meant, literally, "kick the feet to the moon" dive—a Gainer.

European dives were quite different from the American varieties and some were foolishly dangerous, with the arms required to be by the sides rather than protecting the head on entry. Today, this is changed, and rules are more or less standardized all over the world.

The United States women's team had only about a month to work on these dives before the Olympic tryouts were held at Manhattan Beach, New York. Helen Wainwright won the springboard. Aileen placed second in this event, and also placed in high diving from a stationary platform at 27 feet.

It was several days later before the two girls learned that they were to be accepted as members of the Olympic team. A technicality was involved. The United States Olympic Committee had made the decision to allow American women to compete, although some of the members of the committee felt that the Olympics should be purely masculine, because women might have a distracting influence on the male team. Now, the committee really had a problem. They had to decide whether or not to take two "children" on the team—girl children at that!

Aileen had just celebrated her fourteenth birthday. She was still very small and weighed only sixty-five pounds. Helen Wainwright was two months older, and not much bigger than Aileen. The argument went on and on, pro and con. Should "children" be allowed to undertake the responsibility of representing the United States in Olympic competition?

While the committee conferred, the two girls packed and unpacked for the trip, and were so nervously excited they could hardly sleep at night.

Finally, it was decided to include them on the team that was to sail on a chartered American transport. The year 1920 was not the day of jet airplanes, when teams fly to the Olympics just before the opening, with no worry about a layoff during an ocean trip. The voyage to Europe took almost two weeks, and, because of the layoff, it took another two weeks of practice before the team was ready for the Games.

It was interesting, if saddening, to Aileen to see the Belgian battlefields on a sight-seeing trip so soon after World War I. As if to fit the mood, the weather was cold and rainy. It was a hardship for the divers to practice in the icy water, with the wind whipping about them on the platform, but the United States team had little difficulty winning most swimming and diving events.

Aileen Riggin did more than chalk up points for her team when she won the Fancy Diving event. She was the first woman ever to win this Olympic title. The added thrill that followed the victory, when King Albert of Belgium presented her with the Statuette and Gold Medal, made this Olympics the most exciting experience of a career studded with triumphs.

Aileen went on to national indoor diving championships from 1923 through 1925 (10-foot springboard) and the outdoor title in 1923 (10-foot springboard), in addition to her share of national championship glory as a member of the W.S.A. swimming team from 1922 through 1925. But she was at her peak when the 1924 Olympics were held in Paris.

She had won the tryouts quite easily, and had made plans to turn professional if she won the Olympics again. These plans were delayed when Betty Becker of Philadelphia defeated her in the final—a bitter disappointment. The match was close—so close that Aileen went to the dressing room thinking that she had won, only to learn later that she had not. There was one record, however, that came to her. She swam in the backstroke, placed third, and became the only diver to compete in and place in a swimming race in the same Olympics.

Because she wanted to retire from amateur competition as a winner, Aileen decided to postpone her professional debut for a year. Her decision proved to be a wise one when she won the 1925 national springboard diving championship.

At the time when Aileen took the professional step it was a radical one. There were no other girl divers in the professional ranks—Helen Wainwright turned professional a short time later—and not many men. But she found the experience an interesting and creative one. American swimmers and divers were in demand as teachers and coaches in many countries, and she was never without a position in either of these capacities or in giving exhibitions in both branches of the sport.

Swimming and diving were good to Aileen—chiefly in improving her health and strength. Second only to that were the opportunities to travel, meet interesting people and make longlasting friends whom, she says, she might not otherwise have had an opportunity to know.

In 1930, Aileen married Dr. Dwight Dunham Young, of California, and lived in that state until 1945, when her husband, a Navy Commander, died as a result of his war service. They had one daughter, Yvonne, who did not share her mother's love of swimming and diving competition. But she was quite good at water ballet, and the two used to do a little swimming routine together. Yvonne's athletic interests were riding, skating and skiing.

Aileen is now married to Howard W. Soule and lives in Hawaii, where she swims every day.

Being in at the beginning of a new competitive sport for women, contributing to its development, and stimulating young people to become a part of it has been a great satisfaction to Aileen Riggin. The fiftieth state—the land of swimming—could not welcome a finer champion than the girl from Newport who set her star high and rose up to meet it.

WILMA GLODEAN RUDOLPH

[1940–   ]

THEY SAY that records are made to be broken, and break them Wilma Rudolph did when she took the 1960 Olympic Games in Rome by storm. She emerged from this meeting of great champions with three Gold Medals—the first United States women's track star to achieve this honor since Mildred "Babe" Didrikson accomplished the feat in the 1932 Olympics, in Los Angeles.

Others may reach this pinnacle in future Games, but few will do so against the odds that Wilma faced in her preparation to become a track champion; and few will come on the athletic scene with such special gifts.

It wasn't long after Wilma was born, on June 23, 1940—the seventeenth child born to her father by his two wives—in St. Bethlehem, Tennessee, a tiny corn and tobacco community about forty-five miles southeast of Nashville, that she began to suffer childhood diseases. Her parents, Ed and Blanche Rudolph, feared that she might not live very long. An attack of double pneumonia and scarlet fever when she was four years old severely damaged her left leg. Her parents had another worry. Wilma wouldn't eat. "She stayed so skinny," her mother remembers of those days.

Her parents decided to take her to Meharry Medical College, in Nashville. There she was examined, and the doctor told Blanche that Wilma might get back the use of her left leg if she had daily therapeutic massage.

For two years, Blanche Rudolph traveled with Wilma from Clarksville to Nashville—a round trip of ninety miles—on her weekly day off from domestic service. Wilma had heat and water therapy at the clinic. During the rest of the week, when the devoted mother returned home from work, she spent her free time massaging Wilma's leg until her little girl had fallen asleep—and often long after that. She taught the three other children how to massage, so they could take over when household duties demanded her attention. They all took turns, and Wilma's leg had its home therapy four times a day.

When she was eight years old, Wilma was able to walk with the aid of a specially reinforced high-top left shoe. Her disability did not make her cross. "She tried to play," her mother has said. "The other children came and played with her while she sat there in her chair."

When Wilma was eleven, she was able to discard the special shoe. She began tossing a basketball at a loop her brother had put up for her in the back yard. By the time she was in her sophomore year at Burt High School, in Clarksville, she was good enough at the game to score 803 points in 25 games, and set a new record for high-school basketball players in Tennessee.

Her future turned on a basketball tournament in Nashville. A slight limp and tendency to favor her left leg didn't discourage her. Instead, she was going at sports with enormous enthusiasm. Ed Temple, the women's track coach at Tennessee Agricultural and Industrial State University, watched her play and saw in her a potentially great runner. "She has legs like a race horse, and plenty of competitive spirit," he said later, when the young student had graduated from high school and came under his aegis at the university.

Wilma entered competition when the outdoor season opened. Her track and basketball coach at Burt High School, Clinton Gray, was so impressed by her performances that he drove her to the Tennessee State campus during the summers, so she could have the benefit of Ed Temple's guidance. Coach Gray had given her the nickname of "Skeeter" when she was thirteen. "Short for mosquito," he explained. "Always buzzing around."

In June, 1958, Wilma graduated from high school and entered the university. She practiced track zealously, absorbed all of coach Temple's advice and developed, day by day, the technique and skill that were to make her the fastest woman runner in the world.

Only one thing bothered Temple—the same thing that had disturbed her parents. Wilma wouldn't eat enough. "She doesn't eat, and when she does it's junk—hamburgers and pop," her coach complained.

This may have contributed to the fact that Wilma was too ill in 1958 to run during the season. Then, in 1959, she pulled a muscle in her left thigh, during a meet between the United States and the Soviet Union, in Philadelphia. In spite of this injury, she entered the United States Pan American Women's Track and Field trials, National AAU championships, at Cleveland, Ohio, on June 28, and won the 100-meter dash. Then she was entered in the Pan-American Games, to be held at Soldier Field in Chicago from August 27 to September 7. She lost the 100-meter dash by about five feet to Lucinda Williams, a member of the All-Tennessee State University team, but was on the winning 400-meter relay team that was fifteen yards ahead of Panama at the finish.

Trouble still plagued Wilma. In early 1960, she had her tonsils removed and was very ill for several days afterward. It is a tribute to her spirit that, in spite of her physical setbacks, she was ready for the Olympic Games in Rome in September.

Ed Temple was coach of the Olympic track team, and he was proud of her. "She seemed to be," he said, "the calmest person in the United States squad. She's almost lazy. She often goes to sleep between the semifinal and final runs. There's not a nerve in her body. Then she gets over those starting blocks and—boom—all that harnessed energy explodes into speed."

That's just what it started doing on Friday, September 2, 1960, when she won the 100-meter dash in eleven seconds flat —only $\frac{8}{10}$ of a second slower than the men's time. Three days later, she broke the Olympic record for the 200-meter dash in a qualifying heat, and raced home in the final four yards in front to become the first American woman to win the 200. Fanny Blankers-Koen of Holland (1948), Marjorie Jackson of Australia (1952) and Betty Cuthbert of Australia (1936) were the only women to precede her in double wins.

On September 8, Wilma Rudolph anchored the 400-meter relay team, all from Tennessee State. In the order of running, they were Martha Hudson, Barbara Jones, Lucinda Williams, Wilma Rudolph. It was a thrilling victory for this team, and particularly for Wilma, who had to overcome a bad baton pass between Lucinda and herself to race on to the finish three yards in front of the anchor runner on the German team.

Wilma's performance in Rome was so great, her personality so winning that the Russians called her "Queen of the Olympics." She had captured the hearts of competitors and fans of all countries. The French called her *"La Gazelle," "La* Chattanooga Choo-Choo" and *"Le Perle Noir."* To the Italians, she was "*La Gazella Nera.*"

Her classic running form was called "the loosest and the sweetest of them all." The 5-foot-11-inch, 135-pound athlete seemed to flow, with arms pumping rhythmically, rather than to run. Her sweep of the Olympic sprint championships had ended Australia's eight-year reign, when Marjorie Jackson and Betty Cuthbert dominated the field.

Scores of telegrams in many languages poured into Wilma's quarters. On the field, she calmly and patiently signed autographs by the dozen as Italian fans threw their books down to her from the stands.

After blazing to victory in Rome, the new Olympic champion competed in several invitational track meets in Europe. The crowds wanting to get a glimpse of her in Cologne, Germany, were so huge that mounted police had to hold them back. Her shoes were taken off her feet as souvenirs in Berlin and throngs beat on the bus she was traveling in, to draw her attention. Through it all, Wilma Rudolph kept her poise.

She returned to Clarksville to a tumultuous welcome. Mayor William Barksdale greeted her with a large bouquet of roses; the packed streets were draped with bunting and she was given the biggest parade in the history of the town, including a contingent of soldiers from the famous 101st Airborne Division. Parachutists from nearby Fort Campbell, Kentucky, put on a special drop for her. That evening Clarksville's first integrated dinner was held in Wilma Rudolph's honor. Eleven hundred of her friends and admirers poured into the Armory to hear County Judge William Hudson eulogize her. The Clarksville *Leaf-Chronicle* had already called her "an inspiration to the world in general." Coach Temple had said that there was only one fault he could find with the record of the world's fastest woman runner. "Wilma's never been tested since she came into her form. We don't know how fast she can really go."

Judge Hudson had tears in his eyes when he said, "If I can overcome my emotion, I'll make you a little speech. Wilma has competed with the world and brought home three Gold Medals. If you want to get good music out of a piano, you have to play both white and black keys."

Speeches and television interviews kept Wilma busy for some time after her homecoming. She accepted her fame with the same becoming modesty that endeared her to the public when she had accepted her Olympic medals, but it was a fatiguing time. "No matter where I go now, the phone is ringing every two seconds," she said, "but it's not much bother."

Wilma returned to Tennessee State University, to take the courses that would enable her to become a teacher. But track and public relations cut into her schedule of studies in elementary education. Some of her school friends seemed ill at ease with "the champion," and this disturbed her. Equally so did those who, as she expressed it, "bend over backwards to please me. That's not the same as being friends, and it's certainly not the way I want it."

In February, 1961, Wilma returned to competition in the Millrose Games at Madison Square Garden. This was the first time in thirty years that a woman had been invited to participate in the most famous of indoor track meets. To the delight of the audience—mostly male—she won the 60-yard dash in 6.8 seconds (the men's record is 6.1 seconds).

From this meet, Wilma flew to one in Louisville, Kentucky, and won the 70-yard dash in a new world record time of 7.8 seconds. Still another world record was to fall to her when she ran the 100-yard dash in West Germany, on July 19, 1961, in 11.2 seconds.

Wherever she went, she was pursued by telegrams, ringing

telephones, piles of mail and crowds of people trying to see her. There was still the "tumult and the shouting" that had accompanied her Olympic triumphs.

On October 14, 1961, she thought she had found peace and another kind of happiness when she married William Ward of Linden, New Jersey, a student she had met at Tennessee State in 1960. After their marriage, they took an apartment in Nashville and continued to attend their University classes. Then in May, 1962, just before Wilma's twenty-second birthday, they separated and she moved back into a college dormitory.

Her life has not been an easy one since then. In February, 1963, she had an emergency appendectomy and was side-lined for longer than the usual time. She isn't even certain that she will try to make the 1964 Olympics in Tokyo, or whether she will go on with her teaching career, now that she has graduated from Tennessee State. But with all her troubles and uncertainties, she remains gracious and unassuming.

It has recently been written that Wilma Rudolph is going downhill. A champion like this never really goes downhill. She has spirit and determination, and nothing can take her skill from her. Some serious thought given to all the splendid accomplishments of a young lifetime should be enough, finally, to bring this champion back into the sun. That is where Wilma Rudolph belongs, and that is there she will end.

GLENNA COLLETT VARE

[1903–   ]

No one, man or woman, has ever equaled the United States amateur golf championship record of Glenna Collett Vare. She won the title six times, and has been called "the Bobby Jones of women's golf."

Bobby Jones, himself, wrote of her: "In days when masculine players are complaining about the few opportunities to use the wood clubs through the green, it is especially a treat to watch Miss Collett. Her accuracy with the spoon and brassie is to me the most impressive part of her well-rounded game. It is, of course, her way of absorbing to a great extent the disadvantage of length which any woman must suffer against the best males, but as she does it, there is little disadvantage to be noticed."

Glenna Collett probably inherited her athletic talent from her father, George Collett. Although business occupied much of his time—he was General Agent for the Mutual Life of Worcester, in Providence, Rhode Island—he won many major bicycling championships, as a professional. These included the French championship on the day she was born. He also bowled 300 many times, and played a creditable game of handball. He became interested in golf after Glenna was born.

George Collett started his daughter on her way to golf supremacy just before her fourteenth birthday, when he took her to his country club—the Metacomet Golf Club, in Providence, Rhode Island. Glenna had been born in New Haven, Connecticut, but the family moved to Providence when she was six.

Mr. Collett teed up a ball and said to Glenna, "Let's see you hit it." She did—and it seemed to her astonished parent to go a mile! Mr. Collett teed up another ball—and the same thing happened. This was all he needed to see in her the champion that she was to become. Glenna was obviously a "natural," and it was time for golf lessons. Her father took her to his club at every opportunity, to watch her play, practice and to help her polish her game. In the evenings after dinner, she would hit several hundred balls into a golf net in the back yard at home until, finally, she knew every shot in the game as thoroughly as a veteran.

During summer vacations, Glenna played from morning until evening, taking lessons and practicing. When she was old enough to drive, her father gave her a car. This put her on her own, and she seldom missed a day at the club, taking on the older members, and hoping to learn from their experience.

It probably did not go down very well with her parents when she skipped school to play on the Rhode Island team against the Massachusetts teams in the Boston Association matches. But the experience paid off, and, by the time she was seventeen, she was ready for major tournament play.

Glenna entered the national championship in 1919. In this tournament, she saw what was ahead of her. Golf wasn't just a matter of good, even perfect, strokes. Many other things entered into the winning of a championship—nerve control, good physical condition for going the long way over the course, making the impossible shot to win the match, and, above all, never letting down, however great the strain. To make that winning putt when the chips were down meant the combined application of every effective quality that had gone into the contest, from the first tee to the final hole.

Glenna had all that it took to be a champion except experience in title play. This she gained in the 1919 national and the two national championships that followed.

Her 1922 season began auspiciously. She won the North and South at Pinehurst, North Carolina, then went on to success in the Eastern championship, over the Westchester Biltmore course, at Rye, New York, with 246 for three rounds, a record for the event. Many of the golf writers predicted that she had better than an even chance of winning the national, which she had again entered. This tournament was to be played at White Sulphur, West Virginia, four years after her first appearance in the Boston Association matches, when she had been called the "coming champion." During those years, the title had gone to other women, and the term "coming champion" seemed like a burdensome challenge. In 1921, she had failed to win on her third try in the national at the Hollywood Club, in Deal, New Jersey. In this 1922 national, she felt it would be now or never.

Despite her hopes after the Eastern, they wilted when she looked over the field: Marion Hollins, defending champion; Edith Cummings, her most formidable and, incidentally, most attractive rival in tournament play; Mrs. F.C. Letts, Jr.—the "giant killer"; Mrs. W.A. Gavin, an outstanding British player and recent winner of the Canadian championship.

Glenna's hopes rose again, however, when she went around the Greenbrier course in 75. That was the lowest score posted so far, two days before the tournament began. She decided that the secret of this score was the dinner she had eaten the night before: two lamb chops, creamed potatoes and string beans. So every night during the tournament her dinner menu was the same. It was a long time after the tournament before she could face this menu again.

She also decided that the skirt, sweater and hat that she wore on this day of the 75 must have been a lucky combination. She wore the same costume all through the tournament, even though she felt she might be carrying superstition a bit too far!

From eight-thirty in the morning until four in the afternoon Glenna lived in what she called the "nerve-shattering world that only tournament players with championship aspirations know." Her qualifying round with Marion Hollins was so closely fought that she just managed an 81 against her opponent's 83 to win the medal.

After that, the long grind began. Glenna realized that every day was to be harder than the one before. She won her first two preliminaries, and then met Edith Cummings, who was in a confident mood. Their matches, although spirited and hard fought, were always friendly, and were among the most memorable of Glenna's career. This particular one, in the semifinal, was to prove about the toughest she ever had to face in championship golf.

A reporter wrote at the time, "Miss Cummings was determined to win from Glenna Collett. She swaggered along as jauntily as a bullfighter, ready to pounce on any mistakes her opponent made. She was an up-and-coming figure. No handsomer girl ever graced an athletic contest . . ."

Glenna, too, was a striking figure, with her reddish brown hair and clear blue eyes. She carried her well-proportioned five-feet-five inches with poise.

Edith Cummings set the pace for nine holes and was 3 up, but Glenna rallied, and coming up to the 17th they were all even. Then Edith drove into the rough, Glenna made the hole and was 1 up. They prepared themselves for the finish.

As they pitched over a stream to the home green, Glenna's ball landed nearer the cup. She was grateful for that, because the match had tired her. On the way to the green, she paused on the bridge above the stream that wandered through the fairways, and looked down at the trout swimming leisurely among the rocks. She envied them, so unconcerned about the army of spectators following the players above their haven, or of the battle being fought for a championship. When her attention returned to the match, she saw Edith's putt roll past the pin. She hit her own ball within an inch of the cup. Edith laid a partial stymie (this meant a slight chance of getting around her opponent's ball) with her third shot and missed the cup. Glenna putted into the cup and won the match. She had 82, Edith 83. In the meantime, her final opponent, Mrs. W.A. Gavin, had shot a 78.

The morning of the final started well for Glenna. Her long, accurate drives gave her a steady advantage over Mrs. Gavin, and left her opponent twenty to fifty yards behind. Glenna was 6 up at the end of the first 18 holes. The Englishwoman, who had reached the final of the American championship three times, was not in form. She had a 45 for her first nine holes, and, although she steadied during the afternoon play, her morning score was too much to overcome. The match ended at the 14th hole, 5 up and 4 to play for Glenna.

Glenna couldn't believe she had won. For days, her eyes had seen nothing but the little white ball, sailing and rolling over the fairways and greens of the Greenbrier course. Now, for the first time, it seemed, she raised them to the crowd and the beauty of the land around her.

In 1923, Glenna had her good days and her bad days. She

was finding it tough to be a champion. So much was expected of her, and she wanted to live up to it. In the early tournaments of the new year, she won at Palm Beach, then lost in the January Bellair at Philadelphia. In the March Bellair, she lost 2–1 to Mrs. Dorothy Campbell Hurd, the greatest of the early women golfers, in a heartbreaking match decided on the 17th green where Glenna missed a 2-foot putt.

Glenna Collett, who was just twenty, took the honors that went with her championship very seriously. She was well aware of the clash between the champion and "Old Man Reputation." But, looking back, she feels that she didn't have enough sense to know that "a girl merely won the title by being at the top of her game in the major events."

When the time came to defend her North and South title at Pinehurst, Glenna won 5–4 from Marion Hollins in the final match. She went on to win the Eastern at the Whitemarsh Valley course near Philadelphia. The weather was boiling hot, and only Mrs. Hurd, Mrs. Jackson, Alexa Stirling and Glenna were able to break 90. Glenna won from Alexa by 6 strokes. Then came the Buffalo Country Club invitational. She won a thrilling battle in which her final opponent, Audrey Faust, forced her to the 20th hole before she could take the match. She had met her equal off the tee, and not until she dropped a full iron shot into the cup for a birdie 3 was the battle over.

In the late summer of 1923, Glenna won the Canadian championship, and then came the American national. Although it was a bitter pill to swallow when she lost in the third round to Mrs. Clarence Vanderbeck of Philadelphia, who had won the title in 1915, she had a feeling of "relief, relaxation and freedom" with the sudden loss of her title. Of course, she liked being a champion, but it was pleasant to have the pressure off her. Later, she wrote, "One never appreciates the thrill of it (the title) until the crown rests on another's head and the de-throned is forced to step down into the crowded ranks of the 'also rans.'"

Glenna said something else—not after defeat, but at the height of her career—that ought to be "must reading for every athlete who gets above himself: "A golf champion is merely a player who has the knack of hitting the little white ball a bit more accurately than a few thousand others."

With the 1923 season behind her, Glenna forgot defeat and piled up a golf record that is unlikely ever to be equaled, and probably never surpassed. Playing in 60 matches, she lost only one.

In August, 1924, Mary K. Browne was a finalist against Helen Wills in the national singles tennis championship at Forest Hills. Two weeks later, she and Glenna met in the semifinal of the national golf championship at Glenna's home club—the Rhode Island Country Club, in Providence. Mary K., as she was known to many of her friends, was an idol of Glenna's. The latter had met her opponent and seen her fight the coura-geous, though losing, three-set tennis match at Forest Hills. But this did not prevent an all-out battle between the two in this golf contest that ended on the 19th hole.

It was do-or-die on the putt. Glenna's ball lay 3 inches from the cup. Mary K's lay farther back. It seemed an age to Glenna as her opponent addressed the ball, head and body still, and drew back her putter. Glenna's hands grew clammy, and she gripped her club hard. There wasn't a sound from the gallery. Mary K. hit the ball, and Glenna had an instinctive feeling of defeat as it moved slowly toward the cup. Then it rolled on, just to one side of the mark. But here it hit Glenna's ball, car-omed off and dropped into the cup! Mary K. Browne had won.

This was about as bad a break as a golfer can get, but Mary

K. is still Glenna's favorite sportswoman.

Following her 1922 victory in the national, Glenna began spending her winters in Florida, usually at Bellaire. On one occasion, she was playing a match there on a course crossed by railroad tracks. As she came to the tracks, a train approached the fairway. Without hesitation, she took her spoon from the bag and played the ball over the train to the green, astonishing her opponent and scaring the wits out of the passengers in the line of flight!

In 1923, although Edith Cummings won the national, an eminent sports reporter wrote: "Glenna Collett does not fall short of being the finest woman golfer ever developed in America, not excepting Alexa Stirling, three-times winner of the national, or Edith Cummings, present titleholder." But what followed deflated Glenna's ego: "The Providence maiden has one weakness, an underdeveloped combativeness. She doesn't stick her jaw out and cry, 'Let me at 'em,' as does the colorful Miss Cummings. Glenna is inclined in her play to be sociable rather than savage. This is probably why she is so often beaten unexpectedly by inferior players. . . ."

Glenna did get fun out of golf, and her relationship with her opponents was always cordial. She may have had lapses in combativeness, but not sufficiently to prevent her from regaining her national title in 1925, and winning it again from 1928 through 1930 and once more in 1935.

Glenna's most famous match was against Joyce Wethered, of England, in the final of the British championship, at St. Andrews, Scotland, in 1929. Both players were considered to be the greatest in the world. There are those who still maintain that Joyce Wethered was the greatest golfer of all time.

Glenna set a terrific pace when she shot a 41 for the opening 11 holes . . . and ended at the 18th with a 73. A huge crowd, mostly British, followed the players in stunned silence as it appeared that their champion might be beaten. To Glenna, it was awesome and a "little scarey."

In the afternoon, the gallery, even larger now, seemed like a thundering herd bearing down on the two players. Joyce finally wore Glenna down with 4 pars and 6 birdies over ten consecutive holes, and the match ended with the British player the victor on the 17th (35th) green. The players were mobbed and had to be escorted by "bobbies" from the course to the clubhouse.

Glenna's most disappointing defeat was in the 1931 national final in Buffalo, playing against Helen Hicks. She had won three titles in a row, and she wanted to make it four. Also, she had been married recently to Edwin Vare, Jr., an electrical engineer and President of Vare Brothers, and she was particularly eager to see her new name engraved on the cup. She lost 2 and 1, but took her defeat with the grace that made her one of the most popular champions in the game.

Glenna Collett Vare's greatest victory came in 1935, thirteen years after her first national championship, when she beat Patty Berg in Minneapolis, Patty's home town. The gallery was understandably for the "home town idol," and her fans were often distracting in their enthusiasm, but Glenna won 3 and 2.

Perhaps even more indicative of Glenna's superlative quality as a golfer was her victory in the Rhode Island state championship thirty-seven years after she had first won it!

Glenna still plays in golf competition and has a handicap of four. In May, 1963, she was semifinalist in the Philadelphia Championship. Always a fine shot, she also won the Philadelphia trap-shooting and skeet championship.

The reporter who once questioned Glenna's combativeness

overlooked her long-range "will to win," and the indefinable spirit that puts its mark on all great champions and leaves it there for others to recognize and profit by—in meeting obstacles in everyday living as well as in sports contests.

MARGARET VARNER

[1927–   ]

It took Margaret Varner just three years to go from scratch as a squash racquets player to her first of four national singles championships. The feat was not greatly surprising to those who had followed her athletic career, for she is one of the most versatile players of racket games in the world, has enormous physical capacity and innate energy and drive. But the remarkable thing about her accomplishments in squash is that she was twenty-nine years old when she began to play the game.

She had already made her name as a national junior doubles tennis champion and a world champion in badminton when she went to Sargent College, Boston University, in 1957, as an Assistant Professor of Physical Education. On weekends she played field hockey for conditioning. Some of her hockey-playing teacher friends played squash, too, and they persuaded her to try the game. Thus began a career that ended only with her retirement from competition as national champion in 1963.

Margaret Varner was born in El Paso, Texas, on October 4, 1927. Her parents, Dr. and Mrs. H.H. Varner, were interested in sports generally, but they did nothing to push their daughter into athletics. Their most valuable contribution to

97

her career, she feels, was their "quiet encouragement."

She was a sensitive child and, for that reason, a shy one, but her shyness did nothing to impair her natural athletic skills. She took to sports with ease and enthusiasm—swimming, horseback riding, tennis and badminton.

When she was four years old, she entered the El Paso *Herald Post* Kid's Rodeo and rode in the grand entry. Ten years later, she was the girls' Grand Champion, winning the Girls' Calf Roping, Stake Race, Burro Race and others. The age limit for girls' events is fifteen. The year after Margaret won the Grand Championship, she entered only the calf-roping event, which she won, so that someone else would be sure to win the major title.

At nine years of age, Margaret was the youngest person in the United States to have a National Rifle Association Marksman rating. Many years later, an English journalist wrote of her in the *Badminton Gazette:* ". . . rumour has it that she is as handy with a gun and the richness of the Spanish language as she undoubtedly is with the more peaceful Badminton racket. . . . But don't be mistaken, for she is no gunman type. She may have broad shoulders, but that is the extent of any divergence from absolute femininity. Her attractive Southern drawl and the richness of the colour of her hair will certainly dispel any idea of the wild west. The Texan Bronze is fierce only with a poor little shuttle!"

Margaret had decided, when she was a sophomore at the University of Southern California, to major in Physical Education. And little wonder, as it turned out, for it seems that this strong, bronze-haired girl had dedicated her life to sports and to the development of physical fitness and skill in others who might want to pursue their game to the top, as she has done in hers.

It was not easy for Margaret to progress in tennis and badminton in the beginning. She had no coaching and there was little competition in either sport where she lived. Even after she had graduated from Texas State College for Women and taken her M.A. degree in Physical Education, she had a problem. A full-time teaching load and the difficulty of getting leave of absence to play in tournaments was a handicap. But she had the ability, determination and concentration to succeed in spite of this.

She became a member and Captain of the United States Uber Cup (Ladies' International) badminton team in 1957, was again a member in 1960 and captained a United States touring team to South Africa in 1955.

In January, 1958, the International Educational Exchange Service of the Department of State sent Margaret on a six-weeks' Goodwill Tour to Hong Kong, Ceylon, East Pakistan, India and West Pakistan, Burma and Thailand. The purpose of the tour was to "socialize, promote goodwill, and try to raise the standard of the women in these countries." The Cultural Affairs Officer at the American Embassy in each country handled her program, which would have exhausted a woman of lesser energy and determination. She gave clinics and exhibitions in tennis, badminton, swimming and rifle shooting.

In 1958, Margaret was a finalist in the women's doubles tennis championship at Wimbledon—the world's title championship—with Margaret Osborne du Pont, a singles and doubles winner there in former years and many times winner of United States singles and doubles Championships. From 1960 through 1962, Margaret Varner was ranked number one in the Middle States singles and she was a member of the United States Wightman Cup team in the same years. She was manager of the team in 1963.

99

Her opportunity to develop her squash racquets game was all that she could wish for after she moved to Wilmington, Delaware, in 1958, to become educational adviser to the family of William du Pont, Jr. Squash interest flourished there and all the practice she needed was available in the Wilmington and Philadelphia areas. She took lessons frequently from Norman Bramall, the professional at the Cynwyd Club in Bala-Cynwyd, a suburb of Philadelphia. Club matches, inter-city matches and tournaments gave her the competitive experience she wanted.

She took her share of defeats in the learning stages, but they did nothing to lessen her confidence, for she expected them as steppingstones to the championship that mattered most to her—the United States singles.

Margaret Varner went back to the scene of her introduction to squash—the University Club in Boston—to win her first national title in 1960. She had played through the 1959–1960 season undefeated, so the pressure was strong on her. But she came through without the loss of a game.

In 1933, a cup for competition between Great Britain and the United States was donated by the British squash racquets champion, Susan Noel (also a tennis player of Wimbledon caliber) and Elizabeth Wolfe, Captain of the British team. Margaret du Pont, who has become a good enough squash racquets player to win the national senior women's squash racquets doubles championship in 1962, tells this story of the Wolfe-Noel Cup: ". . . . at the end of the national championships in Philadelphia, so much enthusiasm had been generated for an International Team Match that the official invitation from Lady Aberdare, Chairman of the WSRA (Women's Squash Racquets Association), to have such a competition was made. It was presented to and accepted by Miss Eleanora R. Sears (the first United States squash racquets champion), President of the USWSRA. At the same time, Mrs. Wolfe and Miss Noel, as well as Miss Sears, decided to offer a cup for the International Match, to be played for yearly in alternate countries . . . a coin was tossed to see who would offer the Cup, the American lost and so we have the Wolfe-Noel Cup . . ."

The first Wolfe-Noel match, played in February at the Sleepy Hollow Country Club, Scarborough-on-Hudson, New York, was a resounding triumph for the British team, who won 4–1. World War II put an end to the matches until 1949, when it was decided to hold them every other year in alternate countries instead of annually.

Margaret Varner was first named on the team in 1959, just two years after she started to play squash—a record for any aspiring beginner at the game to envy—and won the opening match against England's Dianne Herman 3–0.

During the 1961 season, only one player was able to beat Margaret Varner—Ann Wetzel of Villanova, Pennsylvania. She won everytime they met except in the national championship, when Margaret was again victorious. Ann also had wins over Margaret in 1962 and 1963, but still was unable to halt the champion's successful defense of her title.

Two things stand out to Margaret Varner as the most memorable in her squash racquets career. The first is winning her fourth national title at her home club—the Wilmington Country Club—on February 9, 1963. The best British team in years was competing. She had to play the number three British player, Mary Muncaster, in the quarter-final; the number two, Fran Marshall, in the semi-final, and in the final, Sheila Speight Macintosh, Britain's number one. Margaret's stamina and skill were proven in the final when she came through after fifty-five minutes of play to win 15–10, 15–13, 7–15, 15–10.

Because of the close confines of the squash racquets court,

the rules demand that no player interfere with another while he makes his shot, for interference might lead to injury or an unfair advantage in preventing a winning return; so far more agility, in combination with skill, is required of the squash player than, for example, the tennis player, who has no such limitations in his court covering or in his position in relation to his opponent.

Margaret had all the ability to conform to the rules without hampering any of her skill; and being a fine sportswoman, she never interfered with an opponent. Her only desire in winning was that she could be called the best, without qualification.

The second most memorable thing in Margaret Varner's career is her match play against Betty Howe Constable, the only other player to win the national Squash Racquets championship four times, and considered to be one of the greatest players of the game.

Margaret first played against her in 1959, her initial competitive year, and took a sound beating. But the experience was valuable, and she never missed a chance to watch Betty play and learn much of her championship technique. The two competed again in 1961 and 1962, when Betty was in semiretirement, but was playing every day with the Princeton team. Their meetings created great attention in the squash racquets world because the former champion was playing in very few tournaments. In 1961, Margaret won in four games; in 1962, in five games. These two great champions will never meet again because Margaret has retired from tournament competition.

Margaret Varner is not discontinuing her interest in her fields of sport, however. In September, 1963, she started a part-time job at the University of Delaware, teaching primarily tennis and badminton. Prior to this, she taught a tennis-bad-minton course at Texas Women's University.

She is continuing her hobby of raising Bobwhite quail and chukar partridges, and still finds time to show her hunter, *Coq d'Fran*, in working hunter classes.

Margaret Varner combines the qualities of all outstanding champions, but she has something else in abundance, a quality that not all champions can claim—personality and spirit as fine as her skills.

THERESA WELD BLANCHARD

[1893–   ]

Wʜᴇɴ ᴛʜᴇʀᴇsᴀ ᴡᴇʟᴅ was four years old, her parents gave her a pair of double-runner ice skates. She was offended by the gift and demanded "big girl skates." This was the beginning of the figure skating career of the woman of whom it was said, "Theresa Weld Blanchard is as superb a skater as ever lived."

Until she was about twelve, Theresa skated on ponds near her home in Brookline, Massachusetts, but then she was allowed to harness her pony and drive herself to the Country Club in Brookline, about three miles away. The ice there was cleared of snow and planed, so she could skate many more days than she could on the ponds.

Figure skating in the United States was just beginning to be influenced by the experts in Switzerland, so Tee, as she was called by her family and friends all over the world, was able to begin with the new style without having to "unlearn" very much.

Her father, A. Winsor Weld, was keenly interested in both her progress and the Swiss innovations. Together they worked on these innovations, and they were joined in their enthusiasm by about a dozen other members of the club.

In 1911, Tee's father was instrumental in founding the Skating Club of Boston, which was to hold sessions in the Boston Arena. The possibility of ice skating for six months indoors gave great impetus to the sport, and the popularity of figure skating grew rapidly around Boston.

Mr. Weld's positions as President of the Skating Club and Secretary of the Country Club in Brookline enabled him to do much for the sport and for his daughter's career. Instructors in figure skating were brought over from Germany. They knew something of the new style, though not much more than those they were employed to instruct. But by working together, teachers and pupils were able to develop it.

By March, 1914, Tee was ready for a figure skating competition that was to be held in New Haven, Connecticut. This was called "the first national fancy skating tournament for the United States championship, with competition open to the world." Irving Brokaw, a New Yorker, had gone to Europe, studied skating there and had returned to the United States to lecture on the sport. Through him, the inaugural competition in New Haven was held.

Tee's training in Brookline and at the Skating Club in Boston had given her confidence. She won the ladies' singles and paired with Nathaniel Niles, a prominent tennis player, she was second to a Canadian couple. She also won the waltz with Niles.

Fortunately for her, there were no obstacles in the way of Theresa Weld's progress to the top of the women's figure skating world. After she had won the first championship she entered, she went on to win every North American title for which she was eligible, except the North American Fours. She was United States champion from 1920 through 1924, and, with Nat Niles, won the United States Pair title in 1918 and from 1920 through 1927. Until his death in 1932, Niles was always Tee's partner in Pair and Dance events.

Figure skating suffered severe handicaps at the time of Tee's greatest achievements. There were few pros, and none of them was very experienced. Ice conditions, even indoors, were not up to today's standard. Boots were inferior to those which now give much more support, and skates were not as highly refined. Theresa, her father and others of their figure skating group studied these problems and did everything they could to help improve equipment and skating conditions. The results of this concerted effort are the ideal conditions under which present-day figure skaters perform. To Tee, being in on the innovations was an experience to remember, for, like pioneers in any phase of a sport, she found the progress and growth of hers as exciting as it was important.

For the next few years after the adoption of the new skating style, three women dominated figure skating, and lifted it from the "infant" stage to maturity—Theresa, who had married Charles Blanchard in October, 1920, Beatrix Loughran of New York and Maribel Vinson of Boston. Although there were no great crowds to see them perform then, for the gallery was comprised mostly of friends and relatives of the contestants, those who saw these great artists on the ice were impressed and enthusiastic.

In December, 1921, a group of men formed the United States Figure Skating Association and took steps to control the sport that was spreading like a prairie fire across the country. An agreement was made with the Amateur Skating Union and the "infant" association. Mr. Weld was elected the first president of the Figure Skating Association and he was able to contribute valuable experience to the new organization and to assist in the standardization of the sport in the United States.

In 1920, Tee and Nat Niles went to Antwerp for the Olympic Games. The ice sports were held late in March, in an indoor rink, but they were an integral part of the Games—not a separate division as the Winter Games of 1924 and those of the years following were to become. It was Tee's first foreign competition, and the most interesting and instructive of any she had yet entered.

There were six competitors in the ladies' singles. Tee won two firsts, and a tie for first from five judges. A Swedish skater, Svea Noren, won the other two firsts and tied with her. Figure skating is judged by a complicated system, so another Swedish woman, Mrs. Magda Julin, who had three seconds and two-thirds, won the event. Although a slightly higher mark by one judge would have given her the Gold Medal, Tee was thrilled to have done so well in her first Olympics, and to have won the third place bronze medal for the United States.

The awarding of the prizes was the most impressive experience of the entire Olympics to her. All the winners assembled behind curtains at one side of the rink, and, as their names were called, the curtains parted and they came out, one at a time, and stood at attention while the band played the national anthem of each in turn.

At this time, the United States had a large army base in Antwerp that supplied the Army of Occupation on the Rhine. So the Olympic rink was packed with American soldiers who had spent the week rooting for their compatriot, Theresa Weld. When she came out to get her Bronze Medal from the Crown Prince of Belgium, soldiers jumped onto the ice from various parts of the arena and ran up to her to present her with huge bouquets of spring flowers tied with ribbons identifying their regiments. Nothing like this ever happened to her again. It was, by far, the most dramatic experience of her championship career.

But something else impressed itself very strongly upon Tee. This was the goodwill and enduring friendships that came out of her championship days. In 1952, when she was in Oslo to report the Winter Olympic Games, a lady spoke to her, asking if she was Mrs. Blanchard. As she started to reply, she recognized her questioner as one of a skating pair she had competed against in 1920. They had not met in all the years since then.

Success in figure skating has given Theresa Weld Blanchard friends all over the world, and they have been a particular pleasure to her, since she and her husband have no children.

Tee's position in the early days of figure skating made it possible for her and Nat Niles to persuade the United States Figure Skating Association to appoint them as a committee to start an official publication, and to underwrite it. They began in an entirely amateur way, in her house, but, gradually, it expanded, until it became a thriving business, sponsored by the United States and Canadian Figure Skating Associations. As editor of *Skating*, Theresa Weld Blanchard kept the magazine going for forty years, until her retirement in June, 1963.

In her active skating days, competition was the thing Tee enjoyed most—not necessarily winning, but giving her best performance. When she had passed the competitive age, she judged for almost ten years. These were exciting times for her, too, for new skaters from all over the world came under her experienced eye, and every development in the sport interested her.

As all great champions do, she looks back on her sport, now, with some nostalgia. But she has the satisfaction of knowing that she made two important contributions to it—she helped to give it its start and set its standards, and she contributed to its glory.

HELEN WILLS ROARK

[1906–   ]

THEY CALLED Helen Wills "Little Miss Poker Face" when she first came on the national tennis scene, and no nickname could have better described her court appearance. Only twice in her long and outstanding career did she let her emotions show.

From the time she first won the Pacific Coast junior championship in 1920, at the age of fifteen, at the Berkeley Tennis Club, Berkeley, California, it seemed that nothing could ruffle Helen's composure or her concentration during strenuous practice hours or match play. She moved serenely toward the heights with a purpose so strong that it seemed to keep her apart from other girl tennis players. During a match, she seldom spoke to her opponent, although she was gracious at the end of the contest, when she and her opponent shook hands across the net.

Helen Newington Wills was born in Centerville, California on October 6, 1906. Her father, Clarence Wills, was a doctor, and a tennis enthusiast who played a fairly good game of tennis for fun. His daughter took to the sport from the time he taught her how to handle a racket at the age of nine, and when the Wills moved to Berkeley a few years later, she was recognized as a potential champion by William C. "Pop" Fuller. "Pop" was a retired chemist who had an uncanny eye for perfection in tennis stroke production. He could watch a stroke being made and, instantly it seemed, pick out the flaws.

Under his direction, Helen's game developed so rapidly that the California State and Pacific Coast championships were scarcely a challenge to her. Hard work was part of Helen's development in all aspects of her life. She was an excellent student, intent upon good marks, so she planned her day around classes, tennis and homework.

In 1921 and 1922, the California Tennis Association sent Helen Wills to the Philadelphia Cricket Club, Chestnut Hill, Pennsylvaina, for the national junior championship. She didn't lose a set either year. It was obvious that she was in a class by herself in the junior ranks, and that it was time for her to make her bid for the women's national title.

With pigtails flying and looking like the schoolgirl that she was, in middie blouse and pleated skirt, Helen was an immediate favorite with the Forest Hills gallery when she played in the national singles championship in 1923. Newspaper headlines blazoned victory after victory as she won her way to the final round, where her opponent was Molla Mallory, holder of the title and six times winner of the championship.

Never before in American tennis had there been a more powerful hitter off the forehand than Molla. Her backhand was weak but steady; her service well-placed and steady, but not hard-hit; her net game was nonexistent. It was the forcing forehand that enabled her to run around many backhands and keep her opponent from the net, or frequently pass her opponent with blistering drives when she did come up. Most important, Molla had the heart of a lion and a tremendous "will to win." But Helen had this "will to win," too, and all the other weapons to defeat Molla—an equally powerful forehand, a strong and accurate backhand, an adequate service and net game. She won the match 6–2, 6–2, and the outcome had been obvious from the beginning. Molla simply couldn't cope with the devastating force and placements that faced her; nor could her reputation make the slightest dent on the confidence of her young challenger.

The new champion was seventeen years old. She was destined to win six more national singles titles, and would probably have won nine in all had she defended in 1926 and 1930. She was recuperating from an appendectomy when the 1926 tournament was played; in 1930 she took a rest from the nationals.

When Helen returned to Berkeley in 1923 as American champion, she entered the University of California. Aside from tennis, her greatest interest was art, and this became her major study at the university. Her daily program was very much the same as it had been in high school—attending classes, tennis practice and homework. By now, though, there was time for fun in the evenings, on weekends—sorority and fraternity parties, and other activities of campus life.

In tennis, Helen had a problem to solve—the improvement of her service. Her grip weakened the delivery of this shot. Holding the racket almost as she did for the forehand (palm of the hand behind the handle instead of on top of it), she couldn't get the proper wrist-action in the stroke. In addition, she threw the ball too high, and in waiting for it to come down to the point where she could hit it, she lost power. In daily practice, she worked to overcome this weakness and master the service. Dr. Wills, watching her with "Pop" Fuller from the club veranda, would call out instructions to her on the court beyond. It must have been a frustrating period, for sometimes she looked tired and discouraged when she came off the court with her practice opponent after an hour's concentrated play.

But by spring, 1924, Helen had accomplished her purpose, and she set her first sights of the tennis season on the Olympic Games. As it turned out, this was to be the last time, to date, that tennis was included in the Olympic Games. The matches were played at the Stade Colombe, near Paris. Helen Wills, Hazel Hotchkiss Wightman, Vincent Richards, Richard Norris Williams, 2nd, and Francis T. Hunter were the American team members. Helen won the women's singles final 6–2, 6–2 from Didi Vlasto, a fine French player, but not in the class of her compatriot, Suzanne Lenglen. The latter had long been the leading woman player of the world, but did not choose to enter the Olympics. Vincent Richards won the men's singles; Helen and Hazel Wightman won the ladies' doubles, Hazel and Frank Hunter won the mixed doubles and Vincent Richards and Frank Hunter won the men's doubles.

It was a happy team that went on to Wimbledon, where the unofficial championships of the world are played. The title that is won at this famous tennis center is the "All-England Championship." But, because every tennis nation sends representatives to the tournament, it is considered the world's championship.

Almost everyone thought Helen would win. The only people who didn't were the admirers of Kathleen (Kitty) McKane (later Mrs. L.A. Godfree). These two players met in the final, as expected. Helen won the first set 6–4, went to 4–1 in the second and was four times within a point of 5–1. Kitty McKane drove almost as hard as Helen did, and her net game was better. When Helen went to the net, she was often cleanly passed. When she stayed in the backcourt, she found herself outdriven. Kitty won the second set 6–4. She, too, had a fighting heart, and a great sense of court strategy. As the third set began, it was clear that she knew the surest way to beat Helen, without enduring endless backcourt rallies and wearing down her own strength, was from the net. So she went up on every forcing shot, and by skillful volleying, deftly placed, she took the third and final set at 6–4. Those who saw the match say it was one of the most thrilling ever played on the Center Court.

In the winter of 1926, the match that the tennis world had been waiting for took place at the Carleton Club, in Cannes, on the French Riviera. Suzanne Lenglen was entered in the tournament. Now the most debated tennis question in the United States and Europe—which of these two great players was supreme—could be answered.

On the day of the final that Helen and Suzanne reached with ease, there wasn't a vacant seat in the stands. People climbed trees overlooking the court, hung out of windows and leaned over roof tops to see the match.

When the players came on court, Suzanne was flamboyant in her colorful headband secured by a diamond pin, her scarf and fashionable, finely pleated tennis dress. Helen wore a simple and appropriate two-piece costume. The match began before a tense crowd. Suzanne's incredible accuracy of placement, fleetness of foot, and ability to make winning returns from any position in court, despite Helen's power, won the first set for her at 6–4.

In the second, she had the lead to win by the same score when she went to 5–4, match point. Helen hit a line drive that the umpire and the players thought was out. The players ran to the net to shake hands. The French spectators shouted themselves hoarse, and would have poured onto the court to congratulate their champion if they hadn't been restrained. Then the linesman responsible for calling Helen's drive strode to the umpire's stand and said that he had not called the ball out.

There was bedlam when the umpire announced the linesman's decision and ordered the match continued. It was difficult for both players, for, even though Helen had had a reprieve, it was not easy for her to summon all her concentration after the natural letdown.

Suzanne won the second set at 8–6. After she had proved her supremacy over Helen Wills, she turned professional, so the two great champions never met again.

One of the first of the spectators who met Helen as she came off the court, to congratulate her on a match courageously played and to console her in defeat, was Frederick Moody of San Francisco. He was a tall, attractive friend of Helen's who had joined her and her mother in Cannes before the match. She later married him in December, 1929.

In 1927, Helen Wills was back on the tennis scene, stronger than ever. Opponents were counting games they won from her, never sets. Wherever she played, she won, until her absence from tournament play in 1930 when the English player, Betty Nuthall, won the American championship. She was absent again in 1932, when I won the American title for the first time.

In 1933, we met in the national final. I was as determined to retain my title as Helen was to regain hers. The match was hard-fought. I won the first set 8–6—the only set I had ever taken from her. Helen won the second, 6–3, and the gallery seemed to settle back to wait for her usual victory as I left the court for the ten-minute intermission. Helen remained on court, seated at the umpire's stand.

When we resumed our match, Helen opened with service and went to 30–15 before I won the game. In the second game, she led 30–0 with two irretrievable drives. Then she overdrove, I won the next point and we were at 30–30. I made a winning volley that took me to 40–30. Helen netted a shot, and I was ahead 2–0. In the third game, Helen won the first point on a forcing service. A forehand and a backhand passing shot by me, an overdriven forehand by Helen and another placement by me gave me a 3–0 lead.

It was my serve. I turned to the ballboy and asked for the balls he was clutching as he stared at the opposite court. He simply pointed, and I looked around to see Helen walking to the umpire's stand. I hurried toward her and heard her tell the umpire that she couldn't go on because her leg was causing her great pain.

"Would you like to rest for a while?" I asked.

"No, I can't go on." She seemed upset as she put on her sweater. The referee had come from the marquee to the court to find out what had happened. He said something to Helen that I didn't hear. She shook her head, and he accompanied her from the court.

Helen didn't play again at Forest Hills. But in 1935 she made her bid for her seventh Wimbledon championship. In a preliminary tournament at Beckenham, near London, England's fine Wightman Cup player, Kay Stammers defeated her. In the fourth round at Wimbledon, Fraulein Cepkova took a set from her. Many of the tennis experts wondered if Helen could get to the final. I felt certain she would, for I realized that she was bound to face a few hurdles as she played back into form after a year and nine months absence from tournament play. With every match she was stronger and nearer her top game. I knew, too, that, since Helen had set her mind on winning her seventh Wimbledon, she would be very difficult to beat.

Both of us got to the final. A strong wind was blowing when we went on court for our match. I had been runner-up to her in 1929 and 1932 on this court. Now I intended to be the winner. With a third American championship to my credit, I had the confidence to do it.

Helen went to 3–0, not a very good beginning for me. But I pulled up to 3–3. That was the last game I won in that set as Helen took it at 6–3. In the second set, Helen surprised everyone who was used to her backcourt attack by going to the net. That was all I wanted, and my passing shots gave me the second set 6–3.

There is no intermission at Wimbledon. We went immediately into the third set. I went to 4–2. Helen missed an easy smash at game point for me and I led 5–2. I remember saying to myself, "Don't miss anything," and I didn't miss much. But Helen won my serve and the score was 5–3.

I went to 30–15 against her service, hit a drive down her forehand line that looked like a winner. I thought I had 40–15. The linesman called it out. Although the umpire questioned his decision, he stuck to it, and the score was 30–30. I won the next point for match point, 40–30. After a long backcourt rally, Helen lobbed very high. I watched the ball closely as I went to the net. I was ready to take it at normal smashing height. Then the wind caught the ball, pulling it down and away from me, and when I finally hit it, I was on my left knee. It was an awkward shot. The ball hit the net cord, rolled to the center strap and dropped on my side of the court.

Helen seemed to take new life from that reprieve. Although the games were hard and tensely fought from then on, she won 7–5 in as great a comeback as any athlete has ever made. For the second time, her "Poker Face" gave way to emotion. She threw her racket high into the air as she came to the net to shake hands with me.

In 1938, we met again in a final at Wimbledon. Helen was after her eighth English title. She had played in no American tournaments, so it wasn't too surprising when she lost to the

English Wightman Cup player, Mary Hardwicke, at St. George's Hill, Weybridge. Her defeat by Hilde Sperling at the Queen's Club tournament, the curtain-raiser to Wimbledon, was even less surprising, for Hilde was the outstanding European champion. She and Helen met again in the semifinal at Wimbledon. The match went on for two hours, and it was so boring, with both players hitting interminably from the backcourt, that spectators began leaving the stands before the match was over. Hilde had come within one point of winning the first set, and that was the only exciting moment of the match.

During my quarter-final match against the formidable Polish player, Jadwiga Jedrzejowska, I tore the sheath of the Achilles tendon in my right leg. My semifinal match against Alice Marble didn't help the leg very much, for this wonderful player, who had taken my American championship away from me in 1936, after I had won Wimbledon, ran me all over the court before I could win 6–4, 6–4.

When Helen and I met in the final for the fourth time, I was assured that my leg would hold up for the match if it didn't go on too long. At 4–4, 40–30 on my service in the first set, I went to the net after a deep drive to Helen's forehand corner. She hit one of those short crosscourt dropping drives that had given trouble to so many opponents. I leaped to the ball to volley, landed on my right foot and that was the end of me. Helen ran out the match 6–4, 6–0 and won her eighth Wimbledon singles title, a record that is unlikely to be equaled.

After this victory, she retired from tournament tennis.

Helen is now married to Aidan Roark. Art is still an important part of her life, and she spends much time at her easel. Since she lives in the temperate climate of Pacific Palisades, in southern California, gardening has become one of her year-round hobbies. Her current interest in tennis is to pass on to young and promising players in the area as much of her court experience as she can give, and to play occasionally for fun and exercise.

INDEX

was born in Globe, Arizona, without any intention of becoming a tennis player. In fact, the next several years of her life were spent moving from copper mines to silver mines with her family, and since she was destined to end with something in her hand, she says she is surprised it wasn't a pick!

Helen Jacobs started playing tennis at thirteen, did better in her first tournament than she expected and went on from there through eighteen successive years of competition. The high spots of these years are: winning the American Singles Championship from 1932–1936, winning the championship of the world at Wimbledon in 1936, retiring the famous Seabright Bowl, winning the American Doubles Championship three times, and winning the three tennis championships—Singles, Doubles and Mixed Doubles—in the same year.

In 1962, she was inducted into the Lawn Tennis Hall of Fame at Newport, Rhode Island. Added to this, among the most exciting experiences of these years were being made an honorary member of the San Francisco Press Club and becoming the only player to be made an honorary member of the All-England Club at Wimbledon before winning the Championship. An ever welcome visitor in England, she was presented at Queen Mary's Court in 1935.

But to Commander Jacobs, the most moving experience of all was holding in her hand her first commission in the WAVES. It is the only thing in the world that could have surpassed the crowded years that preceded it. After three years on inactive duty, following the end of the war, Miss Jacobs returned to Navy service during the Korean War.

She is now a Senior Editor on the Book of Knowledge staff at Grolier, Inc., New York City, and has, among her duties, editorship of the Sports Department.